Steve,

Keep being a
difference-Maker

– All the best

Brian
6/23/19

ADVANCE PRAISE FOR *LEAD WITH IMAGINATION*

"In the sterile world of the military, strategy is defined as the successful combination of ways, means, and ends. But those who practice strategy know to be successful; one has to have an imaginative approach (ways) to influence your people (means) and only those two factors will help you reach your dream (ends). Brian Paradis provides art-induced imagination and myriad stories of those he has influenced and who have influenced him to show how dreams come true. This terrific book tackles the 'art' of leadership with stories, humor, love, grace, and selflessness, and Brian has accomplished his mission."

Mark Hertling, Lieutenant General (Retired) US Army, author of *Growing Physician Leaders*

"Brian Paradis exemplifies how love, authenticity, humility, and creativity power truly great leadership. *Lead with Imagination* is a truly inspired blueprint for how to serve others with all of your heart, mind, and soul."

Todd Park, Co-Founder, athenahealth, Former U.S. Chief Technology Officer, White House Office of Science and Technology Policy, and Co-Founder and Executive Chairman, Devoted Health

"This is a book from the front lines of care that is simultaneously practical, visionary, and highly readable. Paradis' passion is enabling the change the health care system so clearly needs."

Michael L. Millenson, President, Health Quality Advisors, speaker, and author of *Demanding Medical Excellence*

"*Lead with Imagination* is filled with unique events the author experienced along his journey to ultimately becoming a true servant leader. He uses impactful, memorable, and heart-felt stories that truly illustrate the imperative for leaders to be vulnerable, curious, and imaginative. This is a 'must-read' both for future and experienced leaders who wish to become 'Leaders of Consequence.' "

Ann Rhoades, President, People Ink, former
Executive VP of People, JetBlue Airways, VP of People,
Southwest Airlines and author of *Built on Values*

"Anyone who understands leadership as a lifelong journey will enthusiastically resonate with Brian Paradis' personal experience as an accomplished health care executive. Paradis generously shares vital and universal lessons in leadership and in life. As leaders, we are at our best to the extent that we are transparent with ourselves and others. Brian Paradis has accomplished both as a leader and as an author."

Joseph Nicosia, Chief Learning Officer,
Kettering Health Network

"Finally, a healthcare administrator who gets it! Brian Paradis clearly understands that leadership, especially leadership in healthcare, is relationship dependent. This book is a notable tool for any healthcare administrator to motivate an organization's caregivers to deliver the most valuable service that we all must depend on at some point in each of our lives. Brian's inspiring anecdotes are the antidote for an unhealthy healthcare system! With humor, love, and compassion, he helps readers discover and share their innate gifts to heal caregivers, patients, and even themselves. A must-read for anyone with the passion to be a catalyst for healing!"

Chuck Dietzen, MD, Physician, Global Health
Advocate, and author of *Pint-Sized Prophets*

"Brian Paradis takes us on an inspiring, humorous and insightful journey that is a must-read primer for anyone who truly **wants to be a great leader!**"

Jason Brown, Co-Founder, CEO and Chief Strategy
Officer of Brown Parker & DeMarinis Advertising

"Deeply insightful, exquisitely written, and one of the clearest, most engaging books in this genre. Visionary and yet immensely practical, it is a quiet wake-up call from business as usual and shows how to drive market share, achieve top of mind awareness and enthusiastic repeat business, using the most imaginative force known to man—love."

Wintley Phipps, Founder and CEO, US Dream
Academy, vocal artist, and author of *Your Best Destiny*

"Brian Paradis offers a thoughtful, well-written, and deeply personal perspective on a much discussed and often poorly understood topic—leadership. The subtitle says it all—*Regaining the Power to Lead and Live in a Changing World*—not by taking control, creating rules, and establishing bureaucracy. Rather, his approach is rooted in engagement, exploration, and discovery in the spirit of what's possible. The structures that emerge facilitate the accomplishment of great things.

"True leadership is not for the faint of heart; it takes courage, an honest look at oneself, and an appreciation of the impact we have on those around us. Brian challenges the reader to look beyond the usual and set the stage to unleash the creative power of those around them. And that requires trust—a quality too often lacking in organizations today.

"Through a process of guided self-discovery, Brian Paradis takes the reader on a journey, challenging widely held assumptions about leaders and leadership. *Lead with Imagination* will be a refreshing challenge for all who come in contact with it."

Rita E. Numerof, Ph.D, President and Co-founder at
Numerof & Associates, and author of *Bringing Value
to Healthcare* and *Healthcare at a Turning Point*

LEAD

WITH

IMAGINATION

Published by Forefront Books.

Interior Design by Bill Kersey, KerseyGraphics
Cover Design by Bruce Gore, Gore Studio Inc.
Cartoon by Justin Oeftger, www.behance.net/JustinOeftger
Mind Map Illustrations by Tony Dottino

Manufactured in the United States of America

9781948677141
9781948677158 eBook

imagination
WORKS MEDIA

LEAD
WITH
IMAGINATION

REGAINING THE POWER TO LEAD
AND LIVE IN A CHANGING WORLD

BRIAN PARADIS

with CURTIS W. WALLACE

DEDICATION

To the executive team with whom I was privileged to journey, who put their own agendas aside and committed to creating something extraordinary...which they did.

To the more than 25,000 caregivers, including staff, clinicians, advanced practitioners, and physicians who each day brought their energy to the calling of serving and loving those around them, including one another, our patients and their families, and our community. I was in awe of you every single day.

To my colleagues in the healthcare industry, who are some of the best people on this planet.

To my partners and collaborators at CSuite Solutions, Imagination Works Media, Wired Coffee Bar, and SeraFuel, you have given me a new place to imagine, create, and innovate.

To so many who have energized, engaged and elevated me along the way. I am blessed and deeply indebted.

To my children and their spouses, you have *so* taught me "what love has to do with it." You are the future of big imagination.

To my wife, Tina, you fully awakened my imagination on the first "sort of" date I had with you, drinking hot chocolate from the Golden Gallon gas station. You are the most "extraordinary" woman I have ever known, a beautiful blend of motion and emotion, my best friend, creative collaborator, and the girl who makes me laugh. I love you *Beyond Z*.

To my God, your **imagination** created the world and your **love** redeemed it. You are my first and last.

CONTENTS

FOREWORD

THERE ARE MANY KINDS OF BOOKS ON LEADERSHIP, THE result of a publishing boom in this niche that has rolled on since the early 1980s. Some are quite useful; many are entertaining. Most are very similar to one another, offering "how-to" advice to aspiring and practicing leaders based either on some academic formulation of leadership or some popular and engaging metaphor, with or without systematic evidence to support the model.

A very few derive their insight from other springs of wisdom, the best from some deeply lived experience of leading that is admittedly anecdotal, but alloyed and much strengthened by systematic observation, experimentation, and analysis. This is such a book.

Here you will meet a young and developing leader, often "in over his head," who was delivered into successively responsible positions in increasingly complex and large organizations. Rather than accept the way of incremental success and safe reiteration of proven practices, he found himself wandering further and further from the safety of commonly accepted practice in search of ways of leading that would yield profoundly improved results. He has been a combination of a scientist, with a huge healthcare system as his laboratory, and an artist, with a complex, distributed juggernaut of a business as his canvas.

Like many before him, he discovered the importance of culture in our organizations, not just to make them more livable, but to yield better long-term results. The stakes, for him and for others, have been high. When hospital systems accept the status quo and perform below their full potential, you can count the cost in human lives. And when young leaders leave the well-worn paths of management to discover and test new ideas in creating extraordinary performance, the system isn't very tolerant of their differences, and not at all of any signs of failure, even on the way to greater success.

An unusual feature of this book is its choice of language and categories. G. K. Chesterton used to emphasize the importance of education as the formation of the categories in which one will think for the rest of his or her life. The challenge with this essentially conserving view of the way we think comes from the pace of fundamental change in our organizational lives. Profoundly new challenges and opportunities are not likely to lend themselves to the categories, the solution sets, invented for an earlier age. Few, though, are willing to create a whole new vocabulary representing new ways of thinking to get to new solutions. When they try and fail, we think of them as eccentrics. When they happen to succeed, they are the artists we remember, the ones who created a whole new movement against which all future work will be measured.

Here the author has offered a new vocabulary of leading beginning with the word "imagination" and gathering a whole new lexicon through which to assess your work and its impact. Words like "love" and "trust" aren't easily brought into the workplace without abandoning the discipline of business results and mission outcomes. Usually the "soft" doesn't survive, driven out by the "hard." In the stories and analyses shared by the author, however, you will see an emerging paradigm of leading that defies the hard and soft categories because it is at once humanizing and results focused.

Read the following pages with a willingness to sample and reflect and test the ideas against your own experience. Good experiments have to be replicated before science recognizes them as valid and legitimately contributing to a model of reality. Evaluate the picture the author renders as you would a new work of art that requires time and reflection to see it for what it is, read in it the messages too subtle for direct discourse, and feel the truth or lack of it. And above all, use your imagination to apply the lessons he offers to your own situation and context.

Sanford C. Shugart

Dr. Sanford C. Shugart has served in senior leadership in higher education for some thirty-five years, the last twenty as the fourth president of Valencia College in greater Orlando, Florida. Recognized by *Washington Monthly* as one of the ten most innovative college and university presidents in America, he has led the college to the top of its industry, winning the Aspen Prize for Excellence for the college and the McGraw Prize in higher education for himself. In addition, Dr. Shugart has served as an active board member of Orlando Health, which he currently chairs, and is a published songwriter, poet, and essayist. He recently published *Leadership in the Crucible of Work: Discovering the Interior Life of an Authentic Leader.*

INTRODUCTION
LONDON: MAY 10, 1940

IT HAD BEEN A PLEASANT, SUNNY, AND WARM DAY. YET BEFORE the day's end, darkness would fall, and the future of Europe and the world would hang in the balance. Nazi Germany had invaded France and with it secured control of Europe, with the exception of Great Britain. At 6:00 p.m., British prime minister Neville Chamberlain resigned and was replaced by Winston Churchill. Soon Britain's entire army would be trapped in Dunkirk, France, and face certain annihilation by Hitler's forces. All objective assessment suggested there remained little hope for the once sprawling and powerful British Empire. Surrender was the foreseeable and sensible future.

But that is *not* how this story ended. Churchill saw a different possibility. In a speech to the House of Commons, he compelled them by saying, "If this long island story of ours is to end at last, let it end only when each one of us lies choking in his own blood upon the ground." They saw what he saw and voted to fight. They saved the world.

No line better summed up Winston Churchill's eloquence than one delivered by President Kennedy upon granting Churchill honorary American citizenship in 1963. "He mobilized the English language and sent it into battle," said the president, quoting Edward Murrow. But there was something that came before the eloquence of Mr. Churchill's oratory that willed a nation to believe in victory: his imagination.

Yes, imagination. It allowed him to *see* what no one else did. You may not realize that between WWI and WWII, Churchill began painting. Many believe that it was the only thing he did purely for himself. His paintings are quite good, consisting of serene pastures, beautiful countrysides, and the sea. I wonder if it was in this creative process of painting these scenes that he learned to *see* beyond the dark moments. Could it be that it so enlarged his ability to cast a vision for a desperate nation that the British people could picture this vision through his words? Is it possible that his ability to lead with imagination made all the difference? I believe the answer is yes.

A few years after I graduated from college I read a book by Max De Pree, the CEO of Herman Miller, the innovative furniture maker, called *Leadership Is an Art.* I have been asking the question, "What does art have to do with leadership?" ever since I made my final highlights and margin notes in this book. For almost thirty years, I have been studying, thinking, and practicing the art of leadership. I am still learning, but one thing has become crystalline clear: the power of imagination in the art of leadership. The compelling combination of *leader* with *imagination* has pursued and obsessed me and led to writing this book, *Lead with Imagination.*

WHY INVEST YOUR TIME AND MONEY IN THIS BOOK?

The world is increasingly complex, knowledge is advancing at an unfathomable rate, and problems seem unsolvable. Our organizations are in near constant and disruptive transition, and the cultures that define them are disconnected, disaffected, and divisive. Too many of us as leaders show up to our work unsure what we are doing and wondering if what we are doing matters. We are smarter than any generation in history. This is not the problem; it is not the reason for our slow progression. The problem is, our imagination is not advancing at the same pace. And that opens the door to opportunity for those willing to step through, willing to take a risk, and willing to *see* what others don't see. I can promise you three returns for your willingness to take this journey (and I have no doubt you will discover more).

First, you will be inspired by the possibilities and strengthened against the challenges. Both are in abundant supply. I have rarely thought of myself as more than average. At times, I have struggled with self-esteem, fear of not measuring up and of failure, laced with old-fashioned shame. If it had not been for a few teachers, a spouse who believes in me, and a chorus of encouraging friends and colleagues, my journey might have been very different. I want to share my story with you so that, whatever your story is, you will rise up, tighten your grip on the possibilities, and push back the challenges.

Second, you will gain power and confidence to imagine, create, and innovate. You may be tempted to say, "I am not any of those." Let me give you hope. I am an accountant, a CPA at that. I have endured all the jokes about how boring and uncreative we are. The closest I am to being gifted in the arts is that I wanted to be a rock star growing up (I still do on some days). And just for the record, I wasn't very good at math either. In fact, I pretty much made Cs and the occasional D. Imagination and creativity are gifts, but not in the way you might think. We are not "gifted" if we are lucky to have them. Let me explain.

There is a long accepted myth that you are either artistic or you are not. The fact is we are all born with innate imagination, creativity, and curiosity. You will discover in this book how to begin recapturing what you have lost. Imagination is a superpower of limitless supply. I want you to use it for the betterment of your leadership and life and to use it with confidence.

Finally, you will release your fullest potential and facilitate the release of potential from those you lead and care about. You will make a difference by all you touch. Through compliance and control, our educational system and corporations have unwittingly participated in the diminishment of our individual and collective imaginations. We learn very early to raise our hand and have the "right" answer. We quickly assimilate to give the teacher the answer she wants to get points on a test, and from kindergarten on we understand you will be marked off for coloring outside the lines.

However, this was good and right preparation for what was to come as we entered the world of work. Corporate bureaucracy has a fundamental element of its design to protect and control resources. Management is prized above leadership. *Lead with Imagination* is about how to lead and how to do it with imagination. It is first about how to be, about character, before checklists and a list of to-dos. You will understand how to release yourself and those you lead from the constraints of the mind's own making and those of our organizations. This is priceless, both in richness of culture and to the bottom line.

AN UNLIKELY JOURNEY

In the spring of 2006 I was asked to lead Florida Hospital in Orlando, Florida. I served as the chief financial officer for the organization, but I had no operational experience. My feelings of personal doubt, the challenges I knew existed within this large and complex organization, and the responsibility for the welfare and futures of over twenty thousand staff and two thousand physicians nearly overwhelmed me. These feelings only intensified as I thought about the people and community we cared for, almost four hundred thousand through our emergency departments, over one hundred thousand as inpatients and including all other services—well over a million people every year.

I found resonance with Frodo Baggins's words from J.R.R. Tolkien's *Lord of the Rings* when Frodo said to his trusted companion, "Sam, what is this tale we have fallen into?" It was within this swirl of thought that I returned in earnest to the power of imagination. I had delivered a commencement address a few years earlier about the power of Churchill's imagination. From my learning journals where I kept a record of my insights and observations, I reviewed the leadership experiences that worked, remembering those moments someone had engaged "all of me" in pursuit of a goal or purpose. I studied anew those wise thinkers and skilled doers who would now provide strong shoulders on which to stand. As some might say, I went back to the old roads to find a new way forward. I was fully engaged in the struggle to take imagination "live" in the complex, life-and-death world that is a modern hospital and healthcare system.

I faced disgruntled people who had important work to do every day but who felt unsupported. They were confused by the management fads and new initiatives that rolled out each year, and they were subjected to high decibels of noise interfering with the most basic communications. I was challenged by the words underlined in my now-tattered copy of *Leadership Is an Art*: "The goal of thinking hard about leadership is not to produce great or charismatic or well-known leaders. The measure of leadership is not the quality of the head, but the tone of the body. The signs of outstanding leadership appear primarily among the followers." These words felt like an indictment, yet they also contained direction.

It is a natural thought process to think people are *in* or *make up* an organization. That is an incomplete thought. The completed thought is: people *are* the organization. Therefore, if you want to build a great organization with a vibrant, caring, and creative culture that consistently innovates and outper-forms competitors, then you have to instill imagination into the collective culture. That is the secret to building the tone of the body. It is also how the extraordinary happens.

Each of us has developed abilities, learned competencies, and dysfunctional tendencies, as well as ineffective attitudes and mindsets. Imagination is the power to turn our ordinary into extraordinary. In a phrase, that is the tale I fell into. This is the story I want to share in hopes it will light a way and that it will spark you to embark on your journey to *lead with imagina-tion* and to live your story fully.

You may struggle to embrace the softness or fuzziness of imagination in a hard and numbers-based business and tech-nology-driven world. Isn't this like the alchemists of old, mixing base metals in a "magical" process in hopes of producing gold? Let me be clear: nothing is harder than creating culture. There is nothing "soft" about it. It requires an authenticity and humility to start, followed by a heavy dose of vulnerability and risk-taking. That is hard for most us if we are honest. Very hard. We become exposed. We have to put ourselves "out there." Our ideas no longer win because we are the leader. They are entered into the "cauldron of debate" where only the "best idea wins." Our fail-ures are highlighted and reflected transparently to those we lead. This is not a quick fix or a walk down easy street. It is more like a relentless slog through the jungle without a map, but with just a compass pointing to true north. You will crash into things. You might get hurt. This is the nature of adventure and this journey. Yet I promise, after you take those first committed steps, it will be exhilarating. The views are breathtaking, and it will be impos-sible for you to go back to leading *without* imagination.

General Gordon Sullivan was a primary inheritor of a US Army in shambles after Vietnam. He has a very deep under-standing of leadership and leadership within an extreme, "hard" environment. The following passage from his instructive book, *Hope Is Not a Method*, punctuates the point:

> Today's problems can be so close, so intense, that they become like blinders. Getting beyond today begins by *imagining* your organization out in the future. Ask yourself 'What could it be?' . . . and then *imagine* your organization in it. Many people seem uncomfortable with this process. They see it as too much art and too little science—as irrelevant theology in a world that has deadlines to meet. It is not. It is how the Army's leaders of the 1970s and 1980s built the Army that was successful in the Persian Gulf War. It is how successful leaders in business, in all walks of life, in fact, operate: by keeping their eyes on today and on the vision—*always moving forward* [emphasis added].

FINAL GUIDANCE

Lead with Imagination is organized into three sections. The first two chapters cover some of the results achieved at Florida Hospital through *leading with imagination* and how my personal story led me to embrace the power of imagination.

The next seven chapters cover the major themes, principles, and learnings through real stories. Unfortunately, we tend to discover the most important truths and lessons through failure. For that reason, many of the stories are about failures, mostly mine. Fortunately for you, you have a chance to learn from them, or at least feel better about yourself. But I warn you, you will most likely need your own crashes to move toward a richer imagination.

The last two chapters are about you from two perspectives. First, are you ready to walk through the door of imagination?

And second, with this new superpower, what will you do to be a difference-maker?

Each chapter begins with a quote to convey a truth as well as inspire you. This is followed by a "Leadership Lyric." The lyric has two purposes: the first is to connect a concept from the arts, be it music, theater, painting, poetry, and so forth to the theme of the chapter; second, it is a summary of the central idea. At the end is a visual mind map to help you capture and retain the elements contained within.

If you want to get the most from reading of this book, I recommend three things. First, review the map at the end of each chapter before you begin your reading. Ask lots of questions as you absorb the stories and insights. Write them in the margins. Each time you pick the book back up scan through some of your questions, playing with possible answers.

Second, try stuff. Test what you are learning. Create your own, new approaches to it. Adapt it and reinvent some of it. Anticipate that some of it won't work. Be curious and explore why it didn't. Have fun with it. Keep a journal of your experiences. Who knows? You may have your own book, blog, or blow-one-away idea.

Third, up your engagement with the arts. There is no shortage of options here. Go to a symphony, a ballet, or a play. See a rock concert, an art exhibit, or read some poetry or prose. The point is to get outside your normal patterns, to explore and experiment, to open your heart and mind, and hone your observational skills.

I close with a few final thoughts as you start the journey. Leadership is about people. People are about stories. So what kind of story or tale are you about to enter into? It's the best kind. It's a love story. Actually, it's a *hard love* story: a story about learning to love your people, learning to love your customers, and learning to love your community. Turns out, love is the foundation and beginning of learning to *Lead with Imagination*.

I think the whole of it is captured in another passage from De Pree's *Leadership Is an Art*: "In a day when so much energy seems to be spent on maintenance and manuals, on bureaucracy and meaningless quantification, to be a leader is to enjoy the special privileges of complexity, of ambiguity, of diversity. But to be a leader means, especially, having the opportunity to make a meaningful difference in the lives of those who permit leaders to lead."

Good luck and God bless. I can hardly wait to hear your stories as you *lead with imagination*.

If we pull this off, we got the biggest slope in the country.

The Art of the "And"

FINDING OUR WAY AT FLORIDA HOSPITAL

> "There is no passion to be found playing small—in settling for a life less than the one you are capable of living."
> —*Nelson Mandela*

LEADERSHIP LYRIC

CREATIVE CONCEPT: YES, AND

There is a powerful concept at the heart of improvisational theater: *Yes, and* replaces *Or*. It is the idea of staying open to any possibility. It creates a tension to facilitate finding or creating a way through the current scene or place to the next.

SUMMARY

We learn early to put more emphasis on the *or*. You can have this or that, but not both. You can have a vibrant, creative, and innovative culture *and* achieve sustained business results. Leading with imagination makes this possible, not easy, mind you, but possible. If we commit to this journey, to live *and* lead in the art of the "*and*," the adventure will change us forever and for the better. Each of us has a story to live, dragons to slay, and a world to change. It matters, now more than ever. Your imagination is the superpower to open the door and sustain your leadership journey.

A JOURNEY BEGINS

I can describe the first time I visited a hospital, sort of. I know I was born in one. In fact, I had a rare condition that required a blood transfusion to survive, so I even had an extended first stay. I just don't remember it. I next visited a hospital when my brother had his tonsils removed. I remember him bragging about all the ice cream he was getting, but not much else.

The first time I truly remember visiting a hospital, I was twelve. My mother was in a coma. I wasn't told much but it was clear that things were uncertain. I tried to take it all in. The room had an odd quietness. People in uniforms spoke in hushed tones, with the silence interrupted by the rhythmic beeping of the oxygen machine assuring my mom had taken her next breath. The space was also sparse: two chairs, a trash can, a single window with the blinds pulled, and multi-colored wires and blue tubes that seemed to come and go in a confusing array. I was overwhelmed and intimidated, and fascinated.

Fast forward some thirty years later. I was leading one of the nation's largest hospitals. In truth, I felt like that twelve-year-old boy all over again. I was overwhelmed and intimidated, and fascinated.

Each time I entered a patient's room, visited an operating room, or walked through the emergency department, I felt those same feelings. This time, those feelings were accompanied by a deep respect for the people who every day provided medical care for the vast needs expressed in and out of the hospital walls. That is why I am humbled to have played a part in the amazing journey of transformation that took place at Florida Hospital over the nine years I was privileged to lead it. I am even more humbled by the team's patience, teaching, and trust in me as I struggled while learning to LEAD WITH IMAGINATION.

SO WHY HEALTHCARE?

With all the attention on HillaryCare, then ObamaCare, to now TrumpCare, you might think this is a book about healthcare. It is not. It is where I have focused my career and calling, and, for the purpose of this book, is the backdrop for dialogue and discovery. It also happens to be a very interesting place full of stories and drama. This likely explains the popularity of television shows like *ER*, *Grey's Anatomy,* and *Chicago Med*. It's often said that a hospital is the most complex organization on the planet. While that is a bold statement, and perhaps, an overstatement (especially with rocket scientists only a short distance away at Cape Canaveral), I cannot come up with an alternative setting more complex in all its moving parts. Hospitals deal exclusively with people—people who are in some form of trauma, crisis, pain, anxiety, uncertainty, or stress. This alone creates an environment with a wide and nearly endless range of dynamics.

You also might be tempted to think medicine is mostly science and should be reasonably straightforward. Did I mention hospitals deal exclusively with people? Each person is different in every aspect of his or her makeup. However, the science and practice of healthcare was designed to meet the needs of the "average person," not the individual. It often looks at men and women the same, and yet we know they are not. Given the uniqueness of individuals and the current limitations of science, overlaid with the explosion of information, shortages of clinicians and physicians, and financial constraints, medicine must, of necessity, also be art. Sprinkle in patient and family expectations and we have the makings for real trouble.

The business models for healthcare are also complex and often confusing. To simplify things, there are three major groups of healthcare customers. Those using Medicare is the first one. As you have already likely assumed, they are the more seasoned and experienced of us. They tend to be sicker and visit more often.

They make up 40 to 80 percent of some hospitals' business. Most hospitals lose money or barely break even on Medicare patients. Medicare generally pays a single price for a specific service. If someone comes to the hospital with a heart attack, a hospital is paid a predetermined price set by the government no matter how long the stay or what other conditions are treated (though some adjustments are made for significant complications).

The second group, where almost all a hospital's profit is made, is the commercial insurance segment. This group is mostly funded through healthcare benefits from employers or by individuals purchasing insurance through the government exchanges. This is where most of us fit, the twenty-five to sixty-five-year-olds. Each healthcare system or standalone hospital must negotiate with these insurance companies to get paid.

The last group is truly what might compassionately be referred to as the least, the last, or the lost. This group includes those on Medicaid and the uninsured. The uninsured group includes a group of hardworking folks who can't afford health-care even though they are employed (about 75 percent of the uninsured, in fact). They make too much income to qualify for Medicaid and so are trapped, in a sense, by the current system. This group often has limited access to healthcare and ends up in the emergency department very sick, often with limited family support or resources to deal with their conditions. They face a range of other challenges, including employment, housing, and food. Hospitals typically incur substantial losses from this customer category. In addition, there are difficult challenges for the staff in delivering effective care, especially after initial treatment or stabilization.

At the same time, healthcare has all the traditional business challenges:

- Managing how much to invest and grow to meet community needs and market opportunities.

- Determining profit targets and budgets to fund that growth, maintain access to loans, and pay down existing debt.
- Deciding between dealing with short-term performance versus making investments in information systems, training and development, and additional people to build capability for the long term.
- Attracting talent in physicians and team members through wages and benefits.
- And, in larger systems, deciding how to balance the local needs of the communities a hospital might serve against the efficiency and scale gained by optimizing the system as a whole across a region or even across states.

Healthcare operates under a vast and often conflicting set of regulation, licensure, and reporting. Often a problem with a single patient will jeopardize the entire operation. I have experienced this on several occasions, and I'll share more later on one of those times. These rules are constantly changing and often don't make sense by the time they trickle down to where patients actually receive care.

The sheer number of procedures, treatments, and locations for service is truly extraordinary in most hospitals. At Florida Hospital, there was almost nothing we could not handle. Everything from treating a broken finger to transplanting a heart and lung were undertaken on any given day. Each weekday, we staffed over ninety operating rooms for surgical procedures.

One morning at 4:30 a.m., I watched a pediatric flight crew take over from the emergency team at our smallest hospital. The emergency physician and nurses had been working on a teenager in cardiac arrest for almost an hour. They had brought this young man back from death. Like a choreographed dance, the flight crew simply slid in from behind and, one by one, took over, packed the patient up, moved him to the helicopter, and up they went for the ten-minute flight to the children's hospital to continue the miracle. Barely any words were spoken, as if they had practiced a hundred times how to do that. I was in complete awe as I watched, and proud that I got to call these caregivers my colleagues.

One of the least understood complexities are the *doctors*. I will likely hear from many of my physician friends, "So, we are complexities now?" (I will joke I have been tempted to call you worse at times.) This humor is a dark humor, reflective of a long history of stressed relationships between physicians and hospital administrations. In truth, doctors are some of the most incredible, hardworking, compassionate, committed, and intelligent people I have ever known or worked with.

However, the ways in which they relate and are organized in a typical hospital defies logic at times. Today many doctors are employed by hospitals. Some physicians are in academic residencies where they must balance teaching with taking care of patients, often with teaching as the first priority. And still other physicians remain in private practice with their own business to run. There are often different motivations, priorities, incentives and clinical practice at work. Yet all these physicians use the hospital's services and, in the eyes of most patients, look like hospital employees wearing lab coats with the name of the hospital stitched right on it. With the stroke of a pen or the click of a keyboard, they decide in the form of an "order" what resources the hospital will expend to deliver care.

This all makes for a very interesting dance. I often counsel young healthcare executives that it is possible to survive bad personnel decisions, upsetting a few board members, missing budget now and then, falling short of patient experience and satisfaction goals, and even making poor quality outcomes (I hate to admit that one). But once you lose the confidence and trust of your medical staff, you should start looking for your next job. While it's an enormous challenge to lead, engage, and manage the medical staff and physicians of a hospital or health system (talk about imagination required), they are the heart, soul, and lifeblood of any healthcare enterprise.

I hope I have convinced you that healthcare is one of the most complex organizations on the planet. And while this book is not about healthcare, if the principles and practices I share in this book produce the transformation and results they achieved at Florida Hospital, they can work for you, wherever you lead.

WHAT IS YOUR PROBLEM?

In 2006 when I assumed my new operating role the healthcare industry was at the beginning of a significant and past-due transition. *Demanding Medical Excellence: Doctors and Accountability in the Information Age* by Michael L. Millenson was published in 1997 and shortly thereafter, the Institute of Medicine (IOM) published a report called *To Err Is Human: Building a Safer Health System.* The message of both of these works, based on a growing body of research, was that each year there were 44,000 to 98,000 deaths due to medical errors in hospitals. Another way to think of it is that 2 to 4 percent of all deaths in the U.S. were caused by hospitals. This was the beginning of the patient safety and quality movement in American healthcare. One of the movements core tenets was that the problem of reducing medical errors and improving patient safety was not solvable at the individual caregiver level. The issues were systemic, caused by the processes or lack of processes in place within hospitals and healthcare ecosystems.

Our organization's first real exposure to this thinking didn't happen until 2005. We were not the early adopters, to be sure, but we were in the second wave. During my first week officially on the job, I joined my new team in the organization's first executive training session on the topic at the Institute for Healthcare Improvement in Boston. This organization was led by Don Berwick, who later become the head of the Center for Medicare and Medicaid Services. They were straight talkers, and it was painful. It was challenging to accept that we might be hurting the people we were supposed to be healing. It was disturbing that, as the senior leaders of the organization, we alone were responsible. Our chief medical officer, Dr. David Moorhead, often described this responsibility as "a sacred trust." He reminded us that if we took a knife and opened somebody up outside of a hospital, it would be a felony. Sobering. The only comfort we found was that we were not alone. This was an industry-wide problem. This problem was the result of many decisions and structures that well preceded any of us at a particular institution or at the industry level. However, we were the ones who had to figure out a way to start fixing decades of mindsets, broken processes, and dysfunctional structures that all contributed to this untenable place in which we found ourselves.

In management and board meetings, I often struggled as the CFO listening to senior executive discussions. The primary dialogues were about money and market share. Most of the hospital administrators had little working knowledge of the myriad clinical processes under their purview. I don't believe we were even aware of these patient deaths except in the most extreme cases. Conversations between clinical and administrative leadership revolved mostly around staffing levels and aberrant physician behavior.

I would often share the observation that at Ford Motor Company, senior executives, talked about cars. Not only did they talk about cars, they talked *passionately* about cars. Where did we talk about our product? Don't get me wrong; I love talking about money, and I really love talking about market share. I am a "grow or die" guy through and through. But market share comes from a great product or service, and I didn't know if we had that or not. As the finance officer, my questions were tolerated and occasionally even appreciated. But they didn't change the dialogue.

Upon assuming the role of COO, I intended to influence this dynamic. During my first year, I realized we had no formal operational business plan, and I thought we needed one. I asked each executive to give me the major themes and goals for their respective areas of responsibility. When I reviewed the clinical care section, it was less than a paragraph. All it said was, "We will continue to deliver good patient care." No measures, no methods, no means. At that point, I understood the deep, deep hole we were in. I wasn't sure if there were a ladder long enough on which to climb out. I knew almost everything had to change. And most of all, I realized people's lives depended on us to find our way.

NOW WHAT?

Imagination was not the first thing that came to mind as we set out to "find a way." In fact, the first thing that came to mind, and the first thing I did, was *apply force*—even brute force laced with a little shame. After all, according to the IOM report, we were hurting people every day in our hospital. Force and shaming were justified. I think I even felt righteous at times, applying these crude and ineffective methods. Today I am embarrassed to admit that. I thought it was obvious that the current ways didn't work. I would regularly suggest a change we needed to make, and the team would raise numerous questions and offer significant challenges to the idea. I became increasingly frustrated, and it began to show in unproductive ways.

I learned a very valuable lesson when I asked a few of my associates why the group wasn't coming along. To my amazement, they told me bluntly, yet supportively, the way I was making people feel. They knew the truth; that was clear. But the way I was forcing them to digest it, without fully engaging them in creating this new future, was difficult. I was not valuing the team or recognizing the systems they were working under. They wanted me to succeed, but they wanted to succeed as well. They wanted to be part of the solution, not just cogs in the organizational wheel simply receiving daily orders from on high.

This led to an idea. A simple one to be sure, but simple is often the most powerful. I decided to talk to more people about what *they* thought. This was a reversal from talking about what *I* thought. I spent the next three months talking with the rest of the executives, with department directors, managers, frontline staff, lots of physicians, patients, and anyone else who didn't run when they saw me approaching with my notebook in hand.

It wasn't always pretty. I particularly remember a group of nurse managers who were hostile and angry. Initially I thought, *Oh my, are we in trouble.* But that was before I listened with my heart and not my head. I realized they were angry because they wanted to do their jobs but the system and we (the senior leaders) weren't helping them. So I dutifully gathered their thoughts about what we needed to do to become a great organization and one they would feel proud to work at. Most importantly, I asked what would make them trust bringing their loved ones to Florida Hospital for care. That question turned out to be a game changer.

Once I completed this work, I shared what I had heard. I validated that I had listened. I asked, "Is this something we as a team could and would commit to? Even if it gets really hard?" As a team we asked if it was simple enough so that we didn't need a stack of PowerPoint presentations to explain it. And we asked if it was compelling. This process led to a five-point map to our future. We named this our Strategic Innovation Agenda (SIA). That agenda was only adjusted once in nine years.

At its center was a powerful idea that we borrowed from Peter Drucker: "The only legitimate business functions were marketing and innovation." Our interpretation into our SIA was "grow the business" (marketing) and "improve the product" (innovation). We debated one more idea at great length. This idea was built on the principle that people *are* the organization. If we don't invest in that as our foundation from the outset, then the outcomes we produce will remain variable. We were reticent to add to Drucker, but in the end, we did. So the final piece of the center framework became "increase our capabilities."

Capabilities were defined by the talent, competency, diversity of thought, resilience, teamwork, and fun in the sinew of the organization's people. We would develop and test it. We would protect the culture from ourselves as the leaders at times, particularly from me. We would be thoughtful about the mission, messaging, and meaning for each person, each work unit, each business line, and the organization as a whole. We also recognized that it was a journey, never a destination. We would strive for this in the long shadow of our humanity and ongoing failures to get this right each day.

It was in this complex, mission-based environment, with a growing sense of the future we wanted, that the idea of leading with imagination began to emerge. It was a hit-and-miss, off-the-GPS, start-and-stop, go-forward-and-then-back-up journey. It didn't happen overnight. It developed out of the willingness as leaders to be open to *seeing*, the trust of teammates to speak their insights and learnings, the willingness to challenge what was, the value placed on one another's contributions to the whole, and the wisdom and commitments that came out of that collective.

What rose to the top among all the good and important parts of creating a fully vibrant, innovative, and high-performing organization are the following seven principles and practices:

1. **Love.** Yes, take a deep breath and take a moment. Let it sink in. Not romantic love nor the holding hands and singing "Kumbaya" that some of us have experienced. As wonderful as those moments are, we are talking about something different. It is love as a principle versus love as a feeling. Even the dictionary struggles with an adequate definition. Perhaps the simplest way to express it in our context is to care as much for one another as you do yourself. There'll be more on this later, but we expressed this organizationally as "love in all interactions." This understanding sets the stage and provides fertile soil for the rest of the principles.

2. **Authenticity with humility.** It's probably worth taking another deep breath, though the effort gets a little easier after this. For most of us, these two requirements will challenge every square inch of our soul. It sure did and still does for me, especially the humility thing. But the payoff for wrestling with this one is the ability to build trust. This trust is nothing short of miraculous in an organization's culture. And culture is "the thing." Trust serves as the lubricant as the enterprise's performance flywheels turn. Trust is a nearly priceless commodity. Combined with love, trust forms a deeply rooted system for leading with imagination.

3. **Painting the canvas.** I told you they would get a little easier. Well, sort of. The best way to describe this is that "everything matters." Yes, everything. The organization is the canvas, and every brushstroke on it makes the painting better and nearer to the vision or takes us away from it. Our work is to make the work environment a place for humans—a place where people feel safe, where they and their opinions matter, and where they have a chance to reach their fullest potentials. Everything matters, from how compensation to bonuses are handled to the propensity for sharing difficult news but trying to spin it all positively.

This principle first requires a thoughtfulness combined both with diligence and persistence in the midst of time and decision pressures. It involves no small amount of courage to speak more of the truth than less of it. It is also about the unintended consequences of actions and symbols, like celebrating individual performance when it really took a team effort, to parking privileges, to the language we use in every forum and type of communication.

It is art and performance in imagining and creating an experience for each person. It is working to develop a genuine harmony, a sense of surprise, and appreciation of the audience, that of the team.

4. **Vulnerability and risk-taking.** As Brené Brown states in her 2012 TED talk, "Vulnerability is the birthplace of creativity, innovation, and change."

So once we are willing to be vulnerable and exposed, there is one more thing we must do. We must take risks if we are to lead with imagination. I have learned much from the military men and women with whom I have had the privilege to journey. They might say it this way: there is no offensive advance possible without being vulnerable and exposed. And the only way to win a battle is to advance. You can't win by only holding a defensive position. The same is true if you want to lead, and even more so if you want to do it with imagination.

5. **Cultivating curiosity.** There are two challenges with this principle. First, we must develop an organizational tolerance for one more question. I have seen leaders with an eagerness to "land the plane." This is natural. It requires some insight to recognize that we might be landing the plane on the wrong runway. Please don't misunderstand. If the plane doesn't land, it will eventually run out of fuel and crash. The pressure is real, and landing the plane is generally a good idea. It's just that we have to think about

the environment we create when we are too impatient with a last-minute question about a plane we think we have landed. The second challenge, and perhaps the more difficult of the two, is to nurture people's innate childlike curiosity, to encourage them to risk asking a "dumb question" and explore something more than the obvious. This principle is about *seeing*. Seeing what isn't visible yet. Seeing the thing that might be completely counterintuitive. And seeing when to let the dialogue continue a little longer. This *seeing* is ground zero for cultivating creativity and innovation.

6. **Finding the fun.** For a rather serious person like myself, and the many other serious people who find themselves in leadership roles, this principle may strike you as odd. One person who taught me the power of fun, laughter, and not taking yourself too seriously (even in a most serious endeavor like healthcare) is my wife. She is the funniest person I know. She has always made me laugh. She can turn the most disastrous situation or day into a well-honed stand-up routine. I observed how laughter made guests in our home feel like they belonged and eager to return. I saw how it lightened the everyday burdens and inconveniences of life and the way it brings people together. Laughter makes us all human. I read the science about how endorphins are released into our bodies yielding improved well-being. I watched how an effective politician or executive would use a well-timed joke to relieve tension in a room.

I don't think most organizations are willing to embrace laughter and fun or understand its power to bring creative culture alive. It is said "it is only a short distance from haha to aha." There is something magic, something childlike, and something uniquely human in humor.

7. **Connect the dots.** This is the capstone concept—the place where, perhaps, the results are most directly experienced in the

organization's performance. It is putting it all together, seeing it all work as a leadership model that can scale and improve the predictability of the results. It is about understanding your company as a living organism and seeing the whole ecosystem working. It often involves being committed to leading as a servant, closing any gaps that open, and clarifying the big why and any other questions. It is all encompassing and will, at moments, be all consuming.

SO, WHAT HAPPENED?

While not immediate, the eventual results were sustained and consistently improved. Like most organizations, ours had lived through too many flavors of the month. People initially responded with skepticism. One of our team members described it like this: "It takes a great effort to get a large flywheel moving, but once it is in motion, it gets easier and easier to keep it turning." That was certainly our experience. This is why courage and persistence are critical to this journey. We were doing things differently. We were tearing down outdated belief structures to rebuild a more certain foundation. We had to unlearn much of what we had been previously taught.

Thankfully, the needle began to move, and then move some more. It was not only our financial results that moved, the corporation's primary measure. We coined the phrase "up and to the right" to signify the way the graphs needed to show our performance in the future. Always up. No flat or unsustained trends. I believe the following is the result of trusting the process, following the principles and practices described above, and being daily present.

I will share the key outcomes in three parts. First, the external recognitions, second, the business accomplishments that gave us directional indicators, and, third, the metrics, because they lie the least in any telling of one's story.

1. **External recognitions:** By 2010, we received the state of Florida's Sterling Quality Award. This award is for all industries. I suspect we were one of the largest organizations in the state to ever receive this acknowledgment. Several surveyors, much out of character and protocol, were in tears as they described what they had experienced over the week observing our teams of caregivers, while validating our submitted application. This was an early test to help us know we were making real progress throughout the core of the hospital's operation.

In 2011, we were awarded the Magnet designation for our newly formed Florida Hospital for Children. It is awarded by the American Nurses Association to hospitals for the "strength and quality of their nursing." We were the first in our community to earn this national recognition. This was almost unimaginable for a brand-new children's hospital. In my career, there are few things of which I am prouder than the work Marla Silliman, the senior executive officer, and Trish Celano, the chief nursing officer, did to launch our children's hospital with incredible talent, clinical excellence, and superb patient experience (with the help of our friends at the Disney Institute, led by Jeff James and the partnership of Walt Disney World).

Two years later, 2013 proved to be a productive year as well. The Institute of Diversity in Health Management awarded us the best overall performer for the year for our diversity and inclusion work for both staff and patients. Our largest hospitals all received an A in a national industry and employer grading system (Leapfrog) for overall safety. We continued to win the most preferred hospital category in the Orlando market with the NRC Consumer's Choice Award.

But the most recognized accomplishment was our number one hospital ranking in Florida for the first time by *U.S. News & World Report*. We had ten programs ranked among the top fifty in the nation. We had gone from having zero ranked programs to having ten. (We maintained the top ranking in the state for the remaining three years I was there.) We immediately followed that by becoming ISO 9001 certified for quality (the largest hospital in the nation to receive this designation). Then we were notified we had been selected as a finalist for the Malcolm Baldrige National Quality Award.

2. **Business accomplishments:** These items are transformational strategies and business development and market successes. First, we successfully deployed over one and a half billion dollars into our community to keep up with the demand for our service offerings and the natural growth of sunny Orlando. These projects were uniformly successful as measured by market, clinical, and financial results. They included a new 350-bed tower that was so successful we had to build out all the extra beds a decade ahead of schedule and new patient towers for almost every one of our eight hospital campuses in the Orlando market. We expanded new consumer-centric outpatient services at existing locations and in several developing parts of town.

We also launched a first for Florida Hospital, which was a serious venture into national-level medical research, a very productive and transformational type of research called "translational research." The idea is to dramatically shorten the length of time it takes to get new learnings from the scientists making a discovery to the clinicians delivering it. The model we created became an approach followed by many others in the country by uniting a large healthcare provider with a world-class research organization. In our case, our partner was the Sanford Burnham Prebys Medical Discovery Institute in La Jolla, California. It is recognized as one of the top research centers in the world.

We also ventured deeper into training surgeons with the launch of the Nicholson Center for Surgical Advancement. This center was soon training over ten thousand physicians a year in cutting-edge, noninvasive surgical techniques and robotic-assisted surgery. This was followed by the development and opening of one of the most high-tech operating rooms in the country, particularly for pediatric epilepsy. It has a magnetic resonance imaging (MRI) machine that slides in on a track during surgery to assist the surgeon to operate with much higher precision than is usually possible. That's very important when cutting into your brain.

We took a lead role for our community by supporting the University of Central Florida, which opened the first medical school in the country in over twenty-five years. This required us to go from one primary-care residency (physician-training certification) to five without any federal funding (which most existing programs receive)—no small feat.

Importantly, we began redesigning what medical care for women should be and began construction on a women's tower with multiple, smaller women's centers to create a network of care. The last and largest project (a women's tower) came online just after I left. And as I mentioned earlier, we turned a collection of services for children into a full-fledged children's hospital that led to an invitation from Johns Hopkins to create the largest pediatric heart program in the world. I could go on, but I won't. The only point is to give a glimpse of what is possible.

3. **Metrics.** I will start with people. We measured employee engagement using the Gallup Q12. We moved from a respectable 4.00 mean score in 2007 to 4.40 in 2013, or the 97th percentile for large organizations (those over 1,200 employees). During this same period, our physician engagement score went from the 35th percentile to the 75th. Most are in private practice and they are often difficult to engage. But they were clearly with us on this journey and played a critical and essential role working alongside our employed physicians as partners.

There is a national measure called HCAHPS (the Hospital Consumer Assessment of Healthcare Providers and Systems). This was the one area where our competition had a huge and seemingly insurmountable lead on us. In 2008, just after this reporting became public, we were at the 51st percentile nationally. In 2013, we were at the 77th and better than our competitor. We did this, as you will see, while growing the number of patients at record levels, the opposite direction of industry trends. I recall being asked by a managing partner of a national accounting and consulting firm how we were managing to do this. I didn't quite have the courage then to name it: imagination.

So, on to service volumes: emergency visits grew from 325,000 to almost 550,000 for a cumulative growth of over 8 percent. Both inpatient and outpatient surgeries were declining when we began our journey, yet each grew by more than ten thousand per year. Inpatient admissions were averaging over twenty-five thousand a year more and still growing. But if I had to pick a single metric, it would be market share. The reason is that market share is the best indicator of whether you are adding value to your patients, their families, and the community, combined with the team's ability to invest in physical structures and operating capacity effectively to meet those needs. We moved from a 7 basis point lead in 2007 to an 18.5 point lead in 2014. Our market share was over 52 percent in a market that had seen only minor market share shifts over the prior decade.

What was most compelling about these recognitions, metrics, and performance indicators was their consistent improvement across virtually all aspects of performance. Gone were the sometimes achieved, sometimes sustained results track record of the past. We grew the business *and* improved our patients' experiences. We improved quality *and* bettered physician- and staff-engagement levels. We built new patient towers *and* launched nationally and internationally recognized programs. All of this required extraordinary planning, team-work, execution, *and* imagination.

A FINAL THOUGHT

As I said previously, metrics can lie, and I have no doubt the ones I have shared may as well (though certainly not by intention). But the one who doesn't lie is the nurse by the bedside. The nurse who, when asked if she works at Florida Hospital, said, "Yes, I do, and I love my job, and I love going to work to care for people."

I have heard this anonymously repeated over and over. It's a far cry from a decade before and from my first days of listening when I found myself the reluctant leader. These stories truly affected me and became the final measure of performance for our leaders.

I recall being asked to join a local community forum sponsored by our mayor about the growing biotech industry in our region. There were two tables, one with a representative from each of the health systems in town, and the other with investor groups from the biotech industry. I deferred to the two other hospital leaders to introduce themselves first. They gave impressive hospital-executive introductions: "I am so and so from this and that. We are a full-service hospital system, the region's only something or other, with many campuses generating a lot of money every year. Blah blah blah." I watched the faces looking for a sign that these things mattered to them. It struck me as I listened that this would be the same as meeting a new person and introducing myself this way: "Hi, I am Brian. I have two cars, a pretty nice house, and a wonderful wife. I also have five kids, and did I mention the cabin in the mountains? My income isn't bad either."

So I took a risk. I followed that nurse's lead. Instead of following the traditional healthcare-executive introduction, I simply said, "Good morning. My name is Brian, and I am from Florida Hospital. We *love* taking care of people."

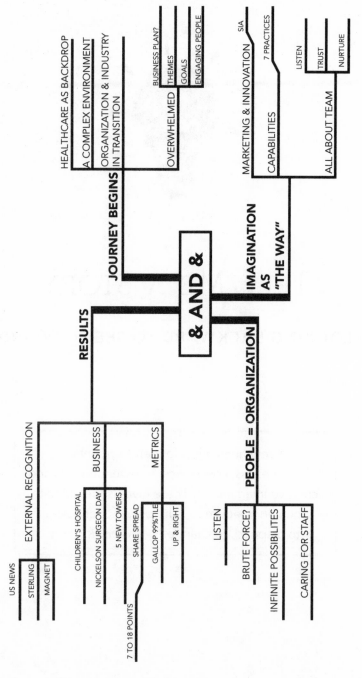

TELL ME A STORY

LOOKING BACKWARD TO SEE FORWARD

"Every human has four endowments—
self-awareness, conscience, independent will and
creative imagination. These give us the ultimate
human freedom . . . The power to choose,
to respond, to change." —*Stephen R. Covey*

LEADERSHIP LYRIC

CREATIVE CONCEPT: NARRATIVE ARC

In literature, this is the story line that typically leads a character through substantial growth and transformation.

SUMMARY

We are the story we tell ourselves. Our world is the one we most vividly imagine. Events and circumstances happen—some we may have influenced and some we haven't. Some may seem difficult, painful, and unfair while we experience others as glorious, energizing, and well deserved. We ultimately choose the meaning, benefit, and the actions we take from these moments. We are not always the originators of the story plot, but we are the authors and creators of the purpose and endings of our story.

PROLOGUE

On my middle daughter's twenty-second birthday, we ordered out, probably Mexican, and were enjoying one of my favorite things: having the whole family gathered around the kitchen table. Inevitably, the highlight of such gatherings in our family comes when one of our five children says something that has everyone crying from laughter. Sometimes it's the same family story that has been told fifty times already but with a new twist, a slight embellishment, or a new detail to make it seem fresh. This time, it was my seventeen-year-old daughter who brought the house down.

"It's all about the story," is one of those phrases I have used on all my kids at various times to encourage personal accountability and taking control of their narrative. (I even tried it on my wife . . . once.) I suspect they would have rightly preferred, at least initially, a little empathy more than counsel. During dinner my son and I were discussing his work managing a group of physician practices. As the discussion became intense and he and I were both getting worked up and leaning into the negative aspects of difficult financial struggles at his company, she chimed in with a grin. "Well Dad, it's all about the story." She was quite pleased to offer this counsel to her older brother and me.

I have been dreading writing this chapter. (Talk about taking control of the narrative.) I don't like talking about myself. I much prefer others to do it. So this morning, as I began my prewriting rituals—the hour-long drive to my writing location, an Americano with two shots of espresso from Island Roasters Coffee in New Smyrna Beach, and a few moments seeking wisdom sitting on a weather-worn and dilapidated dock on the river—I found a peace, of sorts, about what follows.

"It's all about the story."

By this brief telling of my story, in the context of learning to lead with imagination, I hope it adds some color and context to the chapters that follow. I hope that in sharing this story, it will open your eyes to the value of your experience and where your journey has led you thus far. But even more importantly, how imagination desires to take you into new possibilities.

Now, back to our regularly scheduled programming.

OLIVE OIL ON TOAST

I was always a serious kid; I'm not sure why. Maybe I sensed a seriousness in my father and simply emulated that. I don't recall him laughing much, and I suspect watching him work three jobs during the early years of my life may have settled on me in some way.

At the same time, I also had a deep curiosity. I later learned that my curiosity could quickly exhaust the adults in my life. Frankly, I suspect my curiosity *still* exhausts the adults in my life. Of all the instances where my curiosity got the best of me, one in particular sticks out.

Most summers, my parents would send me to visit one set of grandparents and send my younger brother to visit the other set. My mother's parents lived on a beautiful farm in Michigan and were, by most standards, *normal*. You could count on great cooking, cookies, and trips to the old five-and-dime store with an entire basement of toy tractors, cap guns, and other cool toys.

My father's parents, on the other hand, were *unique*. They moved a good bit. Things were often extreme. We might eat the same meal for several days in a row. They didn't eat sugar, so no cookies, pies, or, well, anything a young boy might desire. Trips to toy stores were rare.

Guess where I went most summers?

Exactly. My younger brother won a week of fun on the farm, and I got a week of being *unique*.

My wife has speculated that these summer adventures may explain some of the issues she has keenly identified in my personality as "disorders." For example, I remember early in our marriage when she saw me putting olive oil and a little salt on my toast. She was transfixed by what would cause such an act. Why would I put olive oil on toast with the butter sitting right in front of me? It is simply one of the habits I acquired during those summer visits. That is how my grandfather ate toast because he "didn't believe in butter." However, watching my grandfather do this had taught me that there is more than one solution to the age-old problem of dry toast.

During one of the summers I spent alone with my grandparents, one of the local churches was holding prayer meetings every evening. I wasn't given a choice about whether I wanted to attend. So every night around 5:30, we would get in his car and head across town to the traditional white church building with the prominent steeple at the front. But we always made one stop along the way: to pick up Eli. Eli was a thin, regal, and older black man.

He may have been the first black person I ever spent time with, and he fascinated me. It wasn't because he was black and different than me. It was because of the way he engaged me. He and my grandfather sat in the front seat while I parked myself in the middle of the backseat. I would lean way forward (no seat belts back then), eager to hear every word they were saying and to see the surroundings out of the front window. Eli would ask me questions, and he would answer mine.

I had plenty of questions. Question after question, in fact. One night, it so befuddled my grandfather that he interrupted my questioning for that evening with, "You ask too many questions. You need to be quiet and leave Mr. Eli alone." For a moment, I thought the most interesting part of my summer visit was about to end abruptly. But then, the incredible happened.

Eli looked at my grandfather and said, "Joe, how is a boy to learn if he ain't about asking some questions?"

I reversed my slumping toward the seat to once again leaning forward, questions ready.

Eli finished. "I don't have no problems with his questions, Joe. Do you?"

That evening, during the song service, they sang a song, an old one called "He Lives." There was a line in the song that sounded to me like, "Salvation eating pork." What does eating pork have to do with salvation, I wondered. And what is salvation, anyways? I couldn't wait to ask Eli about this on the way home. With an amused grin, he explained the words *salvation to impart*. I wasn't sure that helped much, but mystery solved. On the other hand, salvation is still a "mystery" I am trying to understand fifty years later.

More importantly, I am still asking questions, and I've learned to embrace my *unique* qualities.

DOWNSTREAM AND DEPENDENT

After struggling to get a degree in accounting I began working as an auditor, first for a church organization and then in a small CPA firm. Next I found healthcare. I was hired by Reading Rehab Hospital in Reading, Pennsylvania. It had been founded about thirty years previously, and a few of the physician founders still came around occasionally. It was a small operation in the idyllic countryside: just one hundred beds surrounded by two hundred beautiful acres. I came to appreciate the position this type of physical medicine rehab held in the healthcare world. It reminded me of the type of rehab facility that had helped my mom so much when I was younger.

Reading Rehab received all of its referrals from the local acute-care hospitals, primarily from orthopedic, stroke, and head-injury cases. Almost 60 percent of our referrals came from one of the three hospitals in town. We knew that it was always possible that one of these hospitals (our referral sources) could decide to build their own rehab hospital. And, in fact, that is what they did about six years after I arrived.

Our CEO, Clint Kreitner, was not from healthcare but rather, the computing world. He understood the business reality we faced and went to work taking the risks that might put us in a better position down the road. One of those risks was hiring me as the controller/chief accountant. I was young, willing to try things differently, and was able to give the occasional candid feedback. In deciding to leave the accounting firm, I had a sense that I was an average accountant with an above-average ability to communicate. This trait had served me well with the firm's clients, and I enjoyed understanding their business. It seemed they appreciated something in our exchanges and in my questions.

During my first few weeks at "The Rehab," I thought to test that theory a bit and try something. I visited with each department head and asked three questions:

- "What do you do?"
- "What are you passionate about?"
- "What can I do to best help and support you?"

The results astounded me. Within a very short time, my boss, the chief financial officer (CFO), shared that he had received numerous notes from various department heads telling him that hiring me was the best decision he had made. This feedback started a chain reaction, reinforcing the belief that there was a different way for the head of accounting to interact with the other leaders beyond just being the guy who crunches the numbers.

A year later, there was a significant reorganization, and I was appointed as the CFO at age twenty-eight. I was in over my head. I knew enough to know what I didn't know. I think the CEO understood that but looked past it and expected me both to learn and think differently about how to face the future, along with the rest of the team. With his support and coaching, I began to try things.

I started with the easiest: financial presentations. In monthly board meetings, the financial reports were often literally read to the audience. I had seen the eyes of some very smart people glaze over only to come back to life when they voted to approve the report. Financial presentations were seen as tedious requirements. The discussions that followed were usually very short.

The idea of accounting as the language of business resurfaced in my head as I thought about this problem. *If accounting was the language, then what story are these financial presentations telling us? How can I convey this story in an entertaining, meaningful, and memorable way? And what will be the result if I am able to engage the board and leadership in better understanding our story, or even rewrite it if we didn't like the one our performance had created?* So, I did something that seemed earthshaking to me at the time: I started my presentation with a cartoon.

Yes, a cartoon. The financial report was serious business. So I thought I would disrupt it just a bit. I knew I didn't possess much skill at humor, so I saw the cartoon idea as a cheat. I figured a laugh might get their attention and help me keep it during my presentation. It helped that I chose a cartoon that conveyed the point I wanted to make as the "headline" or "pull quote" for the current story.

It worked! In fact, the board began expecting the cartoon. Once, in the rush of preparing for a financial report, I forgot to pick a cartoon. The board nearly revolted and suggested I not return in the future without my cartoon. This led to another idea. *If simplifying the way I communicated financial results in our board meetings had such a positive outcome and led to increased understanding, how could I magnify this effect to improve the hospital staff and leadership's understanding of performance as a whole? What other things were in our way?*

WIDENING THE IMAGE

Like most professionals, accountants have a specialized jargon. The problem is that many professionals rely too much on this jargon to demonstrate their expertise and reinforce a position of power. The result is that the jargon separates the professionals from the people he or she should be serving. With this in mind, I rewrote the financial statements. I created a readable format that simply explained the technical terms for liabilities, contractual adjustments, and so on, so that anyone from any department, with no expertise in accounting, could understand them.

Our hospital was part of a network of acute-care hospitals, and we would occasionally be asked to report on our operations to the sponsor organization, a church group. Yet we were different from the other hospitals in the group. We were not owned by the parent organization. We operated under a management agreement. We were also a physical medicine and rehabilitation hospital, not an acute-care general hospital. As a result, we felt a bit like outsiders when we participated in these meetings.

The first time I attended this meeting with my readable financial statement, the other CFOs had no trouble expressing their opinion of my work. Several commented that it read like a "kindergarten" version. They wondered out loud what I was thinking. They were not mean. I just think they honestly did not understand and thought it childish. CFOs tend to speak rather plainly.

The meeting got started, and then the chief operating officer of the church sponsor organization abruptly stopped the meeting and asked a question: "Who prepared this financial statement for Reading Rehab?"

Oh, no.

I felt my face flush and my armpits heat up. I prepared for an uncomfortable few moments. Already feeling out of place as the inexperienced CFO for the odd rehab hospital under a management contract, I responded tentatively, "I did, sir." I braced for impact.

Then he rephrased the question. "I mean, did you write this language for these statements?"

"Yes, I did."

He caught me completely off guard with his next statements. "These are the best financial statements I have ever seen. My ninety-year-old parishioner might actually be able to understand these. And that is very important to me."

Another link in the chain of shaping events.

THE IDEA OF ART

During this time, our CEO led us on an adventure into rethinking what our leadership needed to be about. He asked us to read Max De Pree's *Leadership Is an Art*. It affected me again, partly because I had previously been exposed to the work of Robert K. Greenleaf in *Servant Leadership*. Max's articulation of leadership was deeply coherent with the idea of servant leadership I had embraced. And it affected me partly because he called leadership, which I had thought of as more science and management, *art*.

The idea of art connected with my experience in using story to explain our financial performance. As an executive team, we also explored the concepts of systems theory and its articulation by Peter Senge, Chris Argyris, and Margaret Wheatley. Systems theory is the idea of connectedness and how one action affects other dynamics and outcomes. It was in this crucible of discovery and actions that much of my education in leading with imagination found its first footings.

Clint did one more thing to foster this journey: he modeled much of it. He was uniquely tolerant of our experimenting and encouraging when we didn't quite get it right. As the years go by, the significance of his leadership and influence on me only grows.

WHERE WE BEGIN

As a result of this, my story, I began to think about how understanding art—the process of imagination, creativity, and innovation—might help me think differently about leadership.

This is a part of my story. Each one of our stories is important. They can drive us forward or hold us back. Each of the myriad events in our lives, both big and small, affects the way we communicate, collaborate, and lead. To learn to lead with imagination, we have to accept the baggage we bring with us, leading our organizations as nothing less than complete and yet still-evolving versions of ourselves, as messy as they may be.

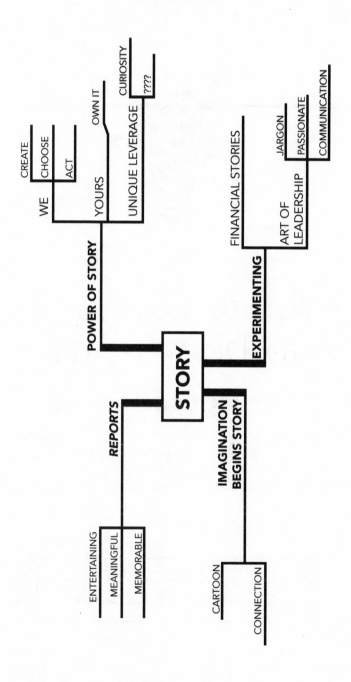

What's Love Got to Do with It?

LOVE IN ALL INTERACTIONS

> "Some people care too much. I think it's called love." —*Winnie the Pooh*

LEADERSHIP LYRIC

CREATIVE CONCEPT: THEME

This is the central idea or point to a story. It frames
the narrative arc and connects with what makes
us human, purposeful, and passionate.

SUMMARY

Love is the foundation, the soil, and the fuel for
imagination. Love is both power and powerful. An
act, service, or business endeavor done in love
universally turns out better. However, love is hard.
It is much easier to give in to fear, cynicism, and
self-interest than to lead, live, and serve with love.

THERE'S ALWAYS A FIRST TIME

The first time I spoke about love as a key driver of our future performance as an organization I almost didn't do it. Our executive team had been growing into this idea over several months. At first it felt awkward, but this team had been together for a number of years and had learned to push the boundaries, so it quickly became comfortable. We had already introduced it to the director-level leadership at our annual planning conference. This group embraced it. It seemed intuitive to them. It was as if they were communicating, "What took you so long?"

Now it was time to start sharing this idea more broadly. First up, thirty-five key physician leaders. I began overthinking. I let fear have its way with me. I started worrying about *my* credibility. These ladies and gentlemen already thought that executives lacked a clue and usually had limited insight into the realities of taking care of patients. This would certainly confirm it.

When I began, I actually apologized for the softness of the concept in the context of the strategy discussion we were having. I explained that I wasn't talking about romantic love or suggesting that we hold hands and sing a verse or two of "Kumbaya." My introduction seems especially awkward in retrospect.

Yet a funny thing happened on the way to "strategy." The doctors never blinked. It made perfect sense to them. I found it makes sense to most people, so it makes one wonder why we don't do it more. You may be tempted to think it makes sense in a hospital but not your business or endeavor. Well, I struggled with it for healthcare. So for the moment, I ask you to stay open, suspend judgment, and consider.

LOVE IS POWER

Love is indeed power and powerful. A friend of mine, Marshall Tarley, served as the chief operating officer of an organization in New York City called the American Society of Composers, Authors, and Publishers (ASCAP). They are the people with whom songwriters register their creative works and who then collect royalty checks for the artists. He shared that there are more than a quarter of a million songs in their database that reference love. If you add their competitor's databases, it almost doubles. He stated, "that without question, 'love' is the most common word in song titles." Love drives us, inspires us, and changes us. It routinely takes center stage and is a narrative theme in all forms of art, music, and literature.

Each year at the Florida Hospital leadership conference, we spent an evening telling stories about our mission in action. It is usually in video form followed by a live interview with the people involved. They are typically patient stories. However, there are also stories of community engagement and caring, or about team members supporting one another through life's inevitable crises. The leaders loved these stories, as they were almost without exception love in action. There was rarely one of these evenings when the entire room of five hundred people wasn't in tears or on their feet clapping. It was impossible to listen to these stories without being affected.

Hopefully, your judgment is still suspended, and you haven't begun playing a tape that says, "Sure, love is great for the arts and healthcare, but you don't understand my business." Probably not, but there is a good chance Sir Richard Branson does. You see, he has created over one thousand brands and numerous companies in industries where love for employees and customers seemed to be in short supply. He says, "There is no greater thing you can do with your life and your work than follow your passions (love) in a way that serves the world and you."

I believe that love gives you power over yourself and your reactions to others, and that love *is* the most powerful force in the universe. However, it doesn't seem that hard to imagine you asking the questions, "What is the power that love would bring to my business, department, or workgroup?" and "How would it transform me, my leadership, and the world around me?"

LOVE IS BETTER

Recently my family moved to Chattanooga, Tennessee. In fact, my wife and three daughters moved the day before Hurricane Irma came right over our soon-to-be-sold house in Orlando, Florida. I stayed to clean up after the storm. It was a Sunday evening when the winds began to howl. I hunkered down in the empty house inside a closet. Around 7 p.m., the power went out. A few minutes later, my phone rang. My wife was calling to tell me something was seriously wrong with our seventeen-year-old daughter and they were on their way to the emergency department. My daughter was jaundiced, listless, and responding to directions slowly and with confusion. After several hours of testing and concerned looks from the ER physician, a shift change occurred, and a new physician entered the room. Without an introduction, he demanded that my wife leave him alone with our daughter.

My wife refused. She is a nurse as well as a mother and was not about to leave our daughter to this stranger. Things raced swiftly downhill from there as he explained he was the doctor and his "word was law." In an attempt to call out his better angel, she shared that she was an evacuee from the hurricane, having literally arrived in town the day before. As she spoke, three of her family members were nearly in the eye of the most massive hurricane most of us have ever experienced. (The eye of the storm was minutes from passing over us in Orlando.) She shared her fear about what was happening to her daughter. Could he please treat her with basic respect?

His response still rings in my ears, and it was not even said to me: "I am not interested in your problems." It was not long after, that at my wife's request the caring staff initiated a transfer to a children's hospital and away from that emergency department and this physician's oversight.

I think we have all experienced a version of my wife's emergency-room experience. We can recall a time when a single encounter with an uncaring person forever altered our feelings about an entire organization. The negative business impact of such encounters can be insurmountable. But the simple infusion of a little love into these same interactions creates a magical and memorable result.

Many organizations spend millions of dollars trying to promote and market themselves, working to get their brand stories right to elicit an emotional connection. But the first and best investment is to love our people within the organization so they can love our customers, or patients, or whomever we serve. Any thoughtful study of Southwest Air and their consistent performance will lead you to a conclusion that this approach is their secret sauce.

Now, consider some of your own stories on both ends of this love spectrum. Who doesn't prefer the "love stories"? Is it that far of a stretch to imagine and then design for them in your organization? What might be the results and the new stories that get told?

LOVE IS HARD

You may be thinking this love thing is a "soft skill." Fair enough. It certainly comes with plenty of nuance and undefined edges. Some of it even fits into the category of "I will know it when I see it." But that does not make it easy. It takes guts, discipline, and a relentlessness to lead with it and develop this culture within your organization or group. It requires leaders to authentically put others first, or, as noted author and popular speaker Simon Sinek says, "Leaders eat last."

I prefer to eat first; I have been to one too many church potlucks toward the back of the line. It isn't always pretty. Many of us have observed or assumed being the leader entitles you to a few perks, like eating first—along with other things including covered parking, better benefits, bigger offices, nicer artwork on the walls, and the list goes on. But love doesn't work this way. It puts others first and so it often doesn't get considered. It is ironic that many in the organizational development and human resource profession would describe love as a soft skill. This language betrays us and keeps it out of our hard business strategy dialogues.

I wish I could say that crossing the finish line with love as an articulated aim at Florida Hospital was the result of a thoughtful dialogue as I've described. It was not. It was more like a stumbling across. We were in the final stages of planning our annual leadership conference. All the presenters for the business sessions were in a conference room going through each presentation with two goals: tightening the messages and connecting the dots so we were integrated to avoid confusing people.

I was going through my part of the morning, the initial setup for the day, the focus and reminders of our big why, and the keys to getting us down the road. I was sharing that one aim of our health system was that we weren't here just to catch people when they were sick or to provide a little bit of prevention or wellness services. It was to help people reach their fullest potential. I next described how we needed to deliver all of our services with compassion. A good thing, to be sure.

One of our senior vice presidents was a retired Lieutenant General. Well, this commander often has feedback, and he barely lost a pace as I was moving through the PowerPoint. He asked, "Shouldn't it be love, not compassion. In fact, shouldn't it be love infused in all our interactions?"

Yes. Yes, it should be.

It took a military general, an outsider to the business of healthcare, a man who has fought and led troops in two wars and who has lived in the hardest of conditions and circumstances, to see it so plainly. Nothing about his experience says the soft or easy way.

I got it. Love is a hard thing. A difficult thing. The right thing!

So what does love have to do with it?

Everything!

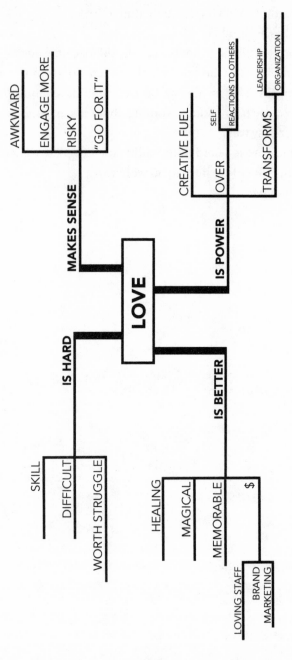

Out of the Comfort Zone

Leaning into Authenticity and Humility

"Whenever I climb I am followed by a dog called 'Ego'." —*Friedrich Nietzsche*

LEADERSHIP LYRIC

CREATIVE CONCEPT: PROSODY

This is a musical idea in which the lyrical content is supported by the musical components of harmony, melody, and rhythm to create meaning. If the lyrical content suggests an emotion of sadness while the musical components pace with energetic rhythm and a soaring melody meaning is confused and likely lost.

SUMMARY

Once you commit to the principle of love, a high hurdle presents itself when leaning into authenticity in your leadership. At the same time, you must become self-aware about the influence your ego casts. Your ego must be managed and medicated. There is not a simple formula for this work. The struggle is the heart of this part of the journey to lead with imagination. It is difficult, if not impossible, to move forward effectively without consistency and balance to your words matching your actions.

WHY ARE HUMILITY AND AUTHENTICITY IMPORTANT?

Merriam-Webster dictionary defines authentic as "not false or imitation" and "true to one's own personality, spirit or character." Humility is defined as "freedom from pride or arrogance." Clearly, that sounds like someone we all would like to know. But they are not the words we most naturally associate with leaders. The question, however, is why does a leader need to possess or develop such traits? Even more to the point, why does character matter?

The answer is trust. While I could argue that this word, *trust*, deserves its own chapter, I will deal with it here because trust is an outcome of our authenticity and humility, as well as the congruency of our actions as individuals and leaders.

In a business, trust works like the oil that keeps the engine of the organization operating smoothly. Like a business, an engine is a complex machine with many moving parts that have to work together and fit perfectly to produce power and motion. However, without oil as a lubricant, the friction from the moving parts of an engine causes the engine to overheat and blow up. The same thing happens with organizations. An organic friction results from the interaction of human beings within a business, a church, not-for-profit, or government enterprise. There must be a lubricant to allow the moving parts—the people—to smoothly interact without overheating. That lubricant is trust.

Trust also functions as a foundation. It is the bedrock upon which to begin building the structures that create and facilitate culture. Once you have a solid foundation with an effective lubricant in the engine that sits on that foundation, you have a safe place to make mistakes. These mistakes are both yours and others. It is in these tolerable mistakes that learning, increasingly creative strategy, more capable execution, and improving performance take root. This has been my consistent experience.

Lastly, there is a price to be paid when trust is not present. Most people are both smart and perceptive (including those people who work for you or with you). If you offer a contrived authenticity or false modesty, there is a high probability you will be detected. When that happens, trust starts to evaporate. Therefore, as you start this journey—if for no other reason than it is simpler and easier and doesn't come with a risk of discovery—start with being who you really are.

Perhaps, if you are being honest, the real you is a little too much like me and many other executives and leaders. We were promoted due to our competence and confidence, weren't we? We have learned the method of feigning support in the boss's meetings, acting the role and saying the right things, projecting an executive presence, and always appearing in control and assured in our answers and directives. Authenticity starts with being honest with yourself first.

By acknowledging your current state to yourself, then to your significant others, followed by a few on your team, you take a great next step toward humility and authenticity. Those around you may not appreciate these traits, but at least they will give you credit for not being a pretender. Oh, and it is likely, that as you begin to take off the masks you wear, believing they keep you from being exposed, you will learn that your staff and team already see through them. The only person being fooled is you.

Margaret Wheatley, in her book *Leadership and the New Science: Discovering Order in a Chaotic World*, describes her learnings about the value of trust: "Power in organizations is the capacity generated by relationships. It is an energy that comes into existence through relationships." She goes on to describe what this learning has led to in her evaluations and assessments of organizations: "I have changed what I pay attention to in an organization. Now I look carefully at a workplace's capacity for healthy relationships. Not its organizational form in terms of tasks, functions, span of control, and hierarchies, but things more fundamental to strong relations. Do people know how to listen and speak to each other? To work well with diverse members? Do people have free access to one another throughout the organization? Are they trusted with open information? Do organizational values bring them together or keep them apart? Is collaboration truly honored? Can people speak truthfully to one another?"

A final thought: this work takes time and patience. It has challenged my sense of urgency often, and it will likely challenge yours. Leaders have an instinct to *get stuff done*, to *take the next hill*. It is far harder to *be* something than to *do* something. But this is the art and essence of leadership: knowing how to *be*, and when to *do*.

DON'T MESS WITH A NAVY SEAL

When I first became the COO of Florida Hospital, I received a memorable lesson in humility and authenticity delivered by Dr. Phil Sanchez. Phil was no ordinary doctor. He was a former Navy SEAL. At least that was the legend that came with him, and I had no reason to question it. He stood nearly six-foot-three. Burly and bearded, he commanded the physical space around him. My family describes me as "smallish," but I prefer "fun-sized." Either way, I was a sharp contrast in stature to Phil. He also possessed a gruff charm and a can-do attitude. Like so many of the exceptional military men and women I have met, an aura surrounded Dr. Sanchez. When he entered the room, you felt it.

Phil had been elected as president of the medical staff, representing the two thousand or so physicians who were part of Florida Hospital. As a result, Phil was my primary partner in the effort to collaborate with the physicians to transform Florida Hospital. My problem was that he scared me. It is hard to admit, but I was flat out intimidated by Phil. Worse, Phil had done nothing to contribute to my fears except be himself. I conjured it up all on my own. Outwardly, I did my best to fake some confidence (not a good example of authenticity), and I even convinced myself the team was buying it. This Navy SEAL, on the other hand, could smell fear a mile away.

It was not long before my intent ran into Phil's military will. It began the day I assumed my new responsibilities and flew to Boston for an introduction to the new and developing disciplines of patient safety and quality mentioned in chapter 1. That dialogue led to hiring a firm specializing in the cultures and processes of patient safety. This was a watershed decision for several reasons.

First, it was expensive, and I was putting my reputation on the line to advocate for this investment. Second, it would likely expose our organization to a harsh reality and challenge many of our assumptions about who we thought we were as a healthcare provider. We had grown accustomed to describing ourselves as good—without rigor or evidence. This could be difficult for leaders above and below. Nobody likes the new guy pulling a bandage off a wound. It hurts and looking at it can be gross. And third, while it's one thing to point out the problems, fixing those problems, especially ones deeply embedded and supported by at least a decade of behavioral norms, is an entirely different dilemma.

From the outset, Phil was enthusiastic in his support of the assessment. He had patient care as his primary concern, not the politics of the organization or medical staff. I promised him transparency with the results once the hospital executive team had digested the report. I was honest with him that I thought it would be a difficult pill to swallow, and I owed the operational team a chance to process it before sharing with our physician leaders. He nodded approval and didn't add much. I walked away pleased with my initial handling, confident I had "maneu-vered" his support.

The assessment was completed over the next month, and the early signals suggested my concerns were warranted. Language like *one mistake away from a disaster* or *leadership and physician culture toxic* were already elevating the stress and suspicions of this work. My own anxiousness about the upcoming meeting with the senior executive and clinical leaders was contributing to some very restless nights.

After one particularly sleep-deprived night, I called Phil on my morning commute to the hospital and reminded him that this first meeting was *internal* only. I rationalized it with him by using the language of a family intervention, reminding him, "You don't invite the cousins and neighbors to watch such a thing." I again committed full transparency, eventually. I was increas-ingly pleased with my handling of Dr. Phil Sanchez, whom I still feared, and the articulate way I facilitated his understanding and support of our process.

There was only one problem. He completely ignored the thoughtful process I had laid out and invited about twenty-five physician leaders to roughly match the number of hospital leaders in the room. Shit! I mean, shoot.

The organizers of the meeting let me know about this develop-ment. Apparently, Phil didn't seem to think it necessary to share this with me directly. It threw a wrench in the meeting-planners' logistics, and they wanted to know from me what they should tell Phil. They actually believed I had the power to tell the medical staff president what to do. Big assumption. I knew I didn't have the courage for this fight, so I casually conveyed a lack of concern or irritation about it. I responded, "It's fine."

The meeting went nearly as planned. It was painful to see this more honest picture of us and the hospital we were so proud of. We saw a picture of dedicated staff who fought through bad processes that mostly got in the way of caring for patients. Our leadership failure was front and center before the culture, from our lack of understanding the clinical processes to our dysfunctional relationship with the medical staff. All the executive team felt this sting. But something caught me completely off guard. My assumptions were in full retreat, refusing to support my decision-making leading to this meeting. It was the physicians' reactions. They felt the failure as keenly as we did, and maybe even more. Huh?

At the conclusion of the meeting, considering what I had witnessed, I did three things. I acknowledged the report and fully accepted the painful result. I honestly shared my own temptation to dismiss much of it and go back to the comfortable world of believing our intentions and beliefs equaled performance. Next, I committed to learning to lead in a new and uncharted world to help make Florida Hospital better by the evidence instead of good because we said we were. I shared a view that greatness is likely never achieved; it is the striving and relentless effort that is important. So the joy for us needs to be in the journey, not the destination. Lastly, I apologized to Phil and the physicians in the room.

"You see," I told them, "I did not want you here today." You could hear a pin drop. I think my team was even more interested in what dark alley their new leader had possibly and unwisely headed into. They were, perhaps, wondering if I really understood how to speak to physicians given my lack of an operating pedigree and personality limitations as a former CFO. I continued sharing how I had negotiated with Phil for a second and later meeting with them. I walked them through my well-intentioned logic of a family intervention, reminding them I had absolutely intended to disclose the assessment.

When I had them set up for the punchline, I concluded. "But I made a grave error that I hope you will be able to forgive me for.

You see, I defined *family* wrong. I saw you as outside the family circle. Somewhere as hospital administrators, we take a class on how to control physicians, and then our language betrays us over and over. I am sorry for this mistake and betrayal. Thank you for being family and caring so much about our patients."

I then confessed to them my fear of the Navy SEAL—to rolling laughter. They knew my fear was misplaced, but they appreciated the obviousness and honesty of my admission standing next to this giant of a man. I thanked Phil for ignoring me and not letting my leadership insecurities keep the doctors in the room from attending. Next, I told these physicians another truth, that executives would likely come and go over the years, but a vast majority of them would practice their entire careers at this hospital, and it was likely more theirs than it was ours. In either respect, it would take all of us to transform it. I was humbled by all I learned that day. I tried to offer an authentic perspective about my actions and my well intended mistakes. But mistakes they were.

That meeting and all that followed set us on a course to challenge what we thought we knew. It began a new covenant with our medical staff. And it moved patients to the top of our concerns. I was humbled by what I missed and how deeply I believed in the "rightness" of what I intended. And yet it was wrong. As evidenced by the appreciation and support of the physicians after the meeting, offering an authentic apology in my wrongness had opened the doors of trust. The lesson from that day still plays like a memorable movie scene in my mind, reminding me of the risk of being too right.

EGO IS A CHRONIC DISEASE

Through my own hospitalization and medical crisis, I gained another important insight. I came to understand that managing the tension between ego and humility is like managing a chronic disease. When I was thirty-nine, I started having headaches when I would ride my bike. I was not a serious rider. The serious riders I knew would spend the several hundred dollars it can cost to be "fitted" to your bike. But I often rode with these serious riders. The rides could range from twenty-five to fifty miles. My self-diagnosis was that my lack of having been fitted must be creating tension in my neck muscles (my left knee often hurt as well) and was resulting in headaches. As my children and wife are keen to remind me, just because I am around doctors every day does not make me one.

My wife, unimpressed with my diagnosis, insisted I ask one of the real doctors I knew what the culprit might be. I did, the day before Thanksgiving 2002. The internist I casually asked after a meeting probed with only one question: "Do you have a family history of heart disease?"

"Yes, but I am thirty-nine, not mid-fifties, when my father had open heart surgery," I answered.

His answer alarmed me. "See a cardiologist and do it right after the holiday."

I did: Dr. Scott Pollack.

We began with what's called a nuclear stress test. Basically they inject a radioactive material in your blood then invite you onto a treadmill, increasing the speed and raising the incline until you think you are going to have a heart attack. Well, at least the doctor is close by. Then they put you under a CT X-ray machine and take a series of pictures following the radioactive material through to your heart to see that everything is flowing smoothly.

During my test, all seemed fine. I didn't even get a headache as I raced on the treadmill.

The next day, the doctor called my cell phone early in the day to let me know I had failed the stress test.

Failed! I hadn't failed a test since eleventh grade Algebra II. And, oh, talk about stress. I had plenty of stress on this job every day. I can handle stress. "Are you sure I failed?" Denial.

"Yes," came the answer.

"Well, what does that mean?"

He was calming in his manner and explained that there is something called a false positive. It was possible that my result was one of these.

"Oh." On the surface, it had a nice ring to it. False *positive*.

He continued to explain that he wanted to do another procedure: a cardiac catheterization. This sounded a bit more ominous, especially when he explained it would not be done in his office but at the hospital. The process involves sticking a long wire through your groin, into a blood vessel, and then snaking it up toward your heart to take a look around via X-ray. Dr. Pollack saw a 98 percent blockage of my right coronary artery. After a short and rather astounding procedure in which they "balloon," or open, the artery and then support it with a metal mesh, I was good as new. Or so I thought.

Three months later, I had intermittent indigestion after eating. Another visit to the cardiologist, another failed stress test, and another mesh stent. This one was just a short distance from the first one. I didn't give it much thought except to think *Okay, now I am good to go.*

Then nine months later, the real chest pain began. I repeated exactly the same process, except this time it was my left artery, what they call the "widow-maker." It still feels like yesterday when I sat on the bottom edge of my bed with my wife's arms wrapped around me. I had just hit the end button on my phone after hearing the news from my doctor of another blockage. We were thinking about our five children, with the latest addition barely a year old. I was fighting tears and the unsettling realiza-tion that I might not be around to watch them grow up. I felt like a failure. They needed me, and yet my body and myself weren't going to be there for them.

I was young. I was not overweight, ate a largely vegetarian diet, didn't smoke, and even got some occasional exercise. However, my vessels were closing at an alarming rate. After several more tests, the likely problem was identified. A part of the fats or lipids that reside in your blood called "LP little a" was about ten times the normal level. The good news was that we had identified the culprit. The bad news was that little is known about this condition. No proven treatment was available. There was only one working theory and, thankfully, that regimen has worked so far, almost fifteen years now. Like many other people, I have a chronic disease. It is not curable today, but it is manageable with consistent, ongoing attention.

I did not intend to grow as a person as a result of this experience. But I did. When you think you are dying, it rather disrupts your views and your world. The Orlando traffic routinely annoyed me so I'd sometimes cut in and out of traffic (don't judge); suddenly that didn't seem like a real problem. It was like using my eyeglasses all day long, then finding myself sitting in my favorite chair, reading and realizing the pages seem blurry. So I take out my eyeglass cleaner and clean them. Then comes that realization: *I can see so much better*. The lenses I saw life through felt much clearer.

But many years later, I wonder how clear that lens still is. In Peter Senge's book *Presence*, he relates a story of a man diagnosed with a terminal disease. The man decides to make the most of the time he has left and begins traveling and living the life that matters most to him. His lens is clear. He even falls in love. This new love encourages him to seek a second medical opinion, which he eventually does. Together, as they sit still and silently in the doctor's office, holding hands as they await the news, they are informed he is *not* dying.

A trickle of tears begins to stream down the man's face.

"Dear, surely these are tears of happiness at this wonderful news."

"No," the man replies, "these are tears for fear I will go back to the life I used to live before I thought I was dying."

I read this passage shortly after I sat on my bed with my wife, wondering about our lost future. I have lived in the reality for the last fifteen years that I have heart disease, a chronic disease. It's not going away. So I must learn to live with it.

It is out of this experience that I came to better understand the way to think about our egos, my ego. Ego *is* a chronic disease. If you don't treat it, it will kill you. When you don't take your daily medicine, it will result in an acute intervention like surgery, or, at a minimum, a frightening visit to the emergency room. You will live with this condition for the rest of your life, and the moment you start thinking or acting like you are cured, it will remind you—in violent and punishing ways—about the falsity of your thinking.

TAKING YOUR MEDICINE

I began sharing this idea of ego as a chronic disease and one of my colleagues said, "Well then, what is the medicine you take for this condition?"

"Well," I answered, "that may be different for each of us depending on the type of disease and severity of it, and our unique genetic makeup, but I will share the medicine I take and take regularly."

I have been learning to say I am sorry—and eventually meaning it. This is almost a wonder drug. It doesn't taste good, mind you. I still hear the song from Disney's *Mary Poppins* playing in my head: "A spoonful of sugar helps the medicine go down." Oh, for a sugarcoated gummy bear version of sorry. I think I would take a couple a day if that were the case.

I also give a few people I trust permission to let me know if they see my condition worsening. In her powerful book *Daring Greatly*, Brené Brown considers people who are sitting on the sideline as critics only. She suggests trusting only the people also spending time in the arena of life and work with you getting muddy and bloody. Choose someone whom you know will be honest with you because not everyone is comfortable or has experience giving feedback. One of those I asked was my chief people officer, Ed Hodge. He saved me from many mistakes with his keen observation and insights. It is also important to reward the person who gives you feedback so they don't feel punished for honoring you with their honesty. What I mean is, if you push back, suggest they don't understand, or point out some flaw in their character or behavior as a "returned favor," they likely won't give you this feedback again. Unfortunately, I have found this to be my natural inclination and have to intentionally fight against this response.

A closely related approach I have had some success with is a series of questions. I like the following questions:

- What can I do better?
- What behavior or new approach would give me a quantum leap in my performance?
- What small change can I implement that would make a big difference in the effectiveness of my leadership and the results I desire?

Experiment until you find the right questions that speak to your heart and soul. In addition, work to find the ones that give the people you chose to ask these questions the most freedom in answering them.

Speaking of soul, I have also found engaging in a spiritual discipline to be most helpful. Whether it is prayer, meditation, service to others, time in nature, listening to uplifting music or experiencing the arts, or anything that serves to elevate your thoughts beyond yourself can be transforming. I have found that spiritual discipline is about listening more than the asking. A purposeful question is useful here, such as, *How can I love more wholeheartedly?* But be prepared to give more of the energy to listening for answers. Give yourself permission to take your time. Don't rush it.

I adopted a willingness to say, "I don't know." In a large and complex operation like Florida Hospital and in a changing world, that answer often is the truth. And yet I have to practice saying it because every part of my being wants to give an answer, sometimes to be helpful and sometimes to suggest it's worth asking my opinion. Sometimes I even guess an answer as though I really know. (I've heard comedians suggest this is a male thing, and given the laughter of both men and women, I think they are right.)

Medicine is both art and science. With this disease, you will need to apply both as well. Experiment, observe the results, and then formulate your personal prescription. Why is it so critical to manage this ego disease and begin the journey to your authentic self? Because to lead with imagination, you need to serve (or eat last, as mentioned in the last chapter). Serving requires your ego to be under control and managed, just as a chronic disease must be.

ARE YOU A SERVANT, A LEADER, OR BOTH?

There are three possible answers to this short question in the context of leading with imagination.

Answer one: you are a servant. This answer is often misunderstood in today's leadership climate. It connotes a certain weakness, or, more crassly, a vision of a doormat or perhaps a passive leader. In the noblest light, a servant more accurately reflects a great strength, a clear purpose, a quiet confidence, and a desire and willingness to put others' needs ahead of your own.

I don't know about you, but this sounds like the kind of leader I would consider following. And, frankly, the best definition of a leader is someone with followers. These descriptions are entirely consistent with the notions of authenticity, humility, and love. So thoughtfully considering this answer is worth your effort and energy.

The second possible answer is that you are a leader. While on the surface this might feel like the natural answer, I would suggest it is incomplete and comes with some heavy liabilities. But what it does have going for it is a common understanding, and even an admiration. Our society has a case of the hero leader. We admire a strong leader. Even if we fear them, we believe they will get things done. He or she will have a direction and we won't flounder. The responsibility for success rests with them, not us, so we don't have to be accountable. This is seductive but does not hold up under scrutiny. There is a long list of organizational and personal failure under this brand of leader.

The Army model offers a poignant picture of servant leadership that starts with a one-to-one, or dyadic model and develops from there. Because healthy feet are vital to a soldier's function and performance, a lieutenant will check each of his soldiers' feet and socks while at the same time learning their family, background, motivations, and more. The young leader is responsible for knowing everything about his squad. They learn about the squad by serving the squad. This story brings to mind another picture from the Scriptures, that of Jesus washing his disciples' feet—the master serving the followers.

This leads me to the third choice: being both a servant and a leader—a servant leader. Early in my leadership journey and my study of imagination, I came across the writings of Robert

K. Greenleaf. He was an early organizational development professional at AT&T. His first published piece was entitled "The Servant as Leader," written in 1970. He was the first to popularize these two words together.

In his thoughtful pamphlet, he laid out a few compelling ideas. He suggests that there is an order to becoming a servant leader. You must first be a servant, willing to put others' needs ahead of your own. This is not unlike the young lieutenant. Then comes the conscious choice to be a leader, often for a purpose or belief. It is when you are pursuing a calling over a career that you have the full capacity to embrace this concept of the servant leader.

Once we understand and commit to leading with love in all interactions, we must dig a deep well of insight, wisdom, and character if we wish to serve and then lead with imagination. The final test, according to Greenleaf, becomes a simple one (which is also in harmony with my experience). Are the people, organization, department, or work unit you lead "better off, healthier, freer, more autonomous, and more likely to become servants themselves"?

This is a high bar, and one worth pursuing. Such leaders change the world, and the organizations they lead perform over the long term. Servant leaders power the organizations that power the world.

NURSES AND THE NIGHT SHIFT

A final story from the place where patients are cared for: the nursing floor. The truth is that nurses in a hospital are often not served well, even as they serve. They are the ones who provide most direct patient care. When a hospital is busy, the nurses have to increase their workload, often to a breaking point. When there is a staff shortage, the nurses will be required to work overtime, often for many days, and sometimes weeks, in a row. Most other functions in the hospital are more stable and are not as affected by cyclical volumes and patient flow as the nursing floor.

Most nurses bear this reality with an amazing grace, possessing a can-do spirit. Our emergency department at the East Orlando campus had experienced a series of record-breaking volume days. I pictured some exhausted and rather cranky nurses taking care of patients. So I thought I should get in my car and check on them. At least I could tell them thank you and, perhaps, give them a pick-me-up that we noticed how hard they were working.

This was not to be. I was the one who left with the pick-me-up. You see, upon entering the ER, I cautiously asked, "How are things going?"

Each nurse I asked had nearly the same response: "We can't help it if people love us." "They know how good we are and how much we care." "Oh, and did you see our patient experience and satisfaction scores?" "We haven't dropped at all. We are just having to communicate that much better about what is going on."

I was past proud and realized they were instructing their leader in some lessons on leadership.

But here is where the operational problem often comes in. When volumes drop, these are the same nurses we send home, either without pay or forcing them to use their vacation days. I didn't like this dynamic. On a practical level, I didn't think it was smart. It is very disruptive to these professionals' financial lives, who are single mothers in many cases. And also, in a profession often marked by shortages, they will start looking for other jobs when this happens too much.

I knew that we had to do a better job of serving and taking care of our nurses. Quickly we changed our systems to require non-nursing areas to take time off if it truly became necessary. This probably didn't make sense on pure work-effort logic, but it certainly sent a message to the nurses that they were not the only ones shouldering this burden. It also created a higher bar to implement the process, since the negative impacts would ripple through more than "just" the nursing units. These other departments were much more vocal when this happened. This process was ongoing and evolving, and we didn't always get this concept of service exactly right. However, the recognition of the problem and the effort to fix it were noticed. Our nurses saw they were valued and that someone cared. The value of that is hard to overstate.

I learned a similar lesson when we implemented some changes to our health benefits. I was pleased because the changes kept the overall premium each employee would have to pay from rising (no small feat in today's healthcare market). However, the changes did have significant financial harm on a few employees who needed expensive drugs or had chronic conditions requiring heavy use of their health benefits. We also made a small change to a group of managers in the nursing leadership structure, effectively moving them from hourly to salary as required by new laws.

As luck would have it, shortly after these changes went into effect our leadership development department was running a training session and the topic of these negative changes came up. It was spearheaded by two night-shift nurse managers who had been significantly affected by both of these changes.

I didn't write a great deal of the communications that went out, but, as bad fortune was still following me, I had personally written the letter that had stirred these two managers. And thanks to their efforts, the rest of the fifty or so frontline managers were now in a heated discussion.

The facilitator called my assistant at a break and asked if I would be willing to address the issue so they could get back to the course they were trying to deliver. I agreed, with little understanding of the dynamic and armed with the conviction that my letter was a good one with a most positive message of no increase in premiums. Upon arrival, I was quickly brought up to speed with a spirited unpacking by one of the two night-shift nurse managers.

She targeted two phrases in the letter to question my integrity. First, they asserted that I had lied in my letter when I wrote, "There would be no increase in your cost" as a result of holding the basic employee premium flat. In their case, that wasn't true. Their premium didn't change, but their cost did go up. Second, in the closing of the letter, I stated that if they had any questions, they should call human resources. To them, that suggested I was not interested, and that I was passing the buck if they had a problem.

As this dynamic was unfolding, several of the executive leaders and others in the room were actively pushing the facilitator, a skilled consultant and trainer, to shut this all down. It was disrespectful to me, and I should not have been subjected to this ambush. They felt strongly I should be protected and not be talked to in this direct and, frankly, accusatory manner. After all, I was the senior leader. While I appreciated their instincts to protect me, that is an example of thinking leader-first. This was a time to be servant-first and care for the wounds of these people.

The two nurses were both affected in real dollar terms, but more importantly, they had lost trust in their leader in a very visceral and personal way. As I was coming up to speak, the poor woman who led the charge was already having second thoughts about her message and delivery style. She half-joked, wondering if she would still have a job after the meeting. I quickly thanked her for having the courage to share so that we at least had a chance to find common ground. I did my best to explain and then apologize for the misstatement as it related to her and the group of others like her who were indeed affected.

Then I just got real about the ending of the letter. I shared that I had given a good deal of thought to it. I did care about making sure they got answers to any questions, but given my inability to take all the calls that might come, I had opted to list the human resources number. I felt it was disingenuous to write, "If you have any questions, give me a call." The entire room nearly erupted at once: "That is exactly what you should have said in the letter!" Who knew? Their message affirmed again that I should have just been authentic and humbly share that I wasn't sure how to close the letter.

I end where I began: authentically making mistakes, and, in humility, saying sorry, asking for forgiveness, and admitting that sometimes I just don't know. This is sacred ground. Tread softly and give yourself permission to fall down, get back up, fall down, and get back up. And repeat. Well, you get the picture. This is the place where you will earn the trust of the people you have the privilege to lead as a servant.

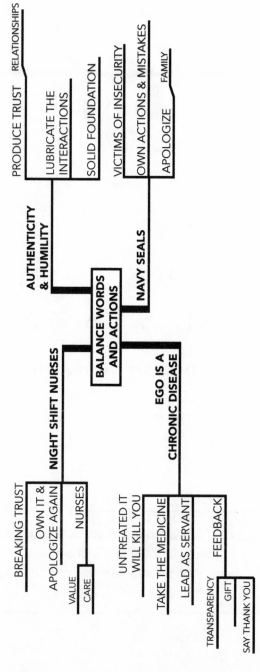

Chaos, Calm, and a Canvas

CREATING THE ENVIRONMENT THAT MATTERS

> "Men occasionally stumble over
> the truth, but most of them pick
> themselves up and hurry off as if nothing
> happened."—*Winston S. Churchill*

LEADERSHIP LYRIC

CREATIVE CONCEPT:
THE SKETCH AND THE STORYBOARD

Leonardo da Vinci sketched the *Mona Lisa* in great detail before he ever put paint to the canvas. Movies, rock concerts, and most creative endeavors liberally use storyboards to visually plan the elements of the work to be produced.

SUMMARY

A leader's primary job is to set the stage, not perform on it. If you want to lead with imagination, you must unleash the power, capacity, and energy of the many and release the stranglehold of the few—even if the few includes you. This is creative work. We often use the language of "creating culture"; however, we don't think enough about what those words mean. This is work that involves careful thought and consideration of every decision we make as another brushstroke applies the paint, either moving us toward a performance masterpiece or moving us away from it.

WHERE DO WE BEGIN?

I wish this work of "creating culture," "setting the stage," or "putting brushstrokes to canvas" was a clean affair. It is not. You don't get to start fresh with a blank canvas. Everyone in an organization brings every bit of their previous "stuff" with them. Their diversity, biases, beliefs, values, assumptions, and fears travel with them. You might say we start with the good, the bad, the ugly, and the beautiful of the people and processes that are the history of all that has come before.

When I think about organizational culture in this way, I am reminded of the reality television show *Bad Ink*. This show follows an incredibly talented tattoo artist in Las Vegas. This guy's talent is his ability to start with a "tattoo disaster" created by another less-than-talented artist and then incorporate that disaster into a new, true work of art. The disaster is still there, but all you can see is the beautiful work of art it has become.

How does he do it? This artist has the imagination to see what couldn't be seen and imagine what could be. He sees how he can use each prior mistake as part of his new work of art. That is the same challenge every leader faces when asked to lead. You must use your imagination and *see* what could be, skillfully using the effective structures and mindsets that are already in place and painting through or over that which does not move you to a better outcome.

THE BEGINNING OF A FRAMEWORK

I have found it's helpful to think about an organizational environment in two parts. The first is the environment you create in the spaces and places you occupy and with the team or teams you lead. There is a leadership reality that you are being watched nearly all the time. You have probably already connected the dots from the last chapter and realized that this is why authenticity is so foundational to leading with imagination. The second part is the company or organizational *gestalt*. This includes the combinations of broad communication, policies, branding, leadership systems, and decision-making structures.

There are numerous overlaps and influences between these two parts. The flow or cascade from the culture you create between you and your direct team is powerful in shaping the company culture, yet it can be both undermined or reinforced by corporate communications as illustrated by the night-shift nurse story from the last chapter. Both of these spheres of effort must be integrated and harmonized to begin to build an effective foundation and framework for the vibrant, creative, and innovative culture *and* the performance needed to thrive.

Still another way to describe this, though often overused, is that you must create a learning organization. Why? People. In the words of General Gordon Sullivan, a former Chief of Staff in the Army, "In the final analysis, everything comes back to people. People are not *in* the organization, they *are* the organization. The bricks and mortar, machines and computers are there only to leverage the power of those people . . . it is the people in your organization that make the difference." Perhaps this feels cliché. It is definitely repeated over and over. But it is rarely understood and executed consistently.

CHAOS: WHEN ART AND SCIENCE COLLIDE

One of the learnings I have applied to creating culture is that of field theory. This is a concept borrowed from the world of quantum physics and chaos theory and applied to leadership and organizations. I was first exposed to its potential applications almost twenty years ago by Margaret Wheatley in her book *Leadership and the New Science*.

She explains that what appears to be solid is, in fact, not. What? Yes, solids are made up of many particles, and there is space between those particles. If your mind is still in one piece and not blown, super. If it is blown, just go with it for another moment. The application she makes to organizational theory suggests that there is also space in the culture of an organization. If you are not pro-actively putting something into that space, others will.

I will let her words articulate it further:

> In a field view of organizations, we attend first to clarity. We must say what we mean and seek for a much deeper level of integrity in our words and acts than ever before. And then we must make certain that everyone has access to this field, that the information is available everywhere. Vision statements move off the walls and into the corridors, seeking out every employee, every recess in the organization. In the past, we may have thought of ourselves as skilled designers of organizations, assembling the pieces, drawing the boxes, exerting energy to painstakingly create all the necessary links, motivation, and structures. Now we need to imagine ourselves as beacon towers of information, standing tall in the integrity of what we say, pulsing out congruent messages everywhere. We need all of us out there, stating, clarifying, reflecting, modeling, filling all of space with the messages we care about. . . . Let us remember that space is never empty. If it is filled with harmonious voices, a song arises that is strong and potent.

Her view supports the adage, "Culture eats strategy."

I was overwhelmed the first time I attempted to absorb her thought stream. I read on, looking for the twelve-step program

I could implement. This made sense to me conceptually, but to achieve this would be unending and exhausting. We might spend so much time, energy, and resources on this that the business itself might be neglected and suffer. But a counterintuitive thought would not relent: build culture before strategy. I couldn't help but feel supported by Jim Collins in his book *Good to Great* with his articulation of getting the right people on the bus.

A second truth would also not relent: if you are the leader, then lead. I needed to take responsibility for my leadership. I had observed in myself and others that the most significant obstacle to building innovative and high-performing cultures was, oddly enough, the leader. One reason was the pressure on a leader to have answers—not just answers, but answers that were *right*. Ken Robinson states, "The role of a creative leader is not to have all the ideas; it's to create a culture where everyone can have ideas and feel that they're valued." At Florida Hospital, we morphed this into a mantra of "best idea wins."

Unfortunately, every organization is different, and you will have to thoughtfully find a path to get you where you determine to go. If you have a mission statement, a vision statement, and a set of core values that are truly reflective of the desires of the organization and resonate with your people, that is a very good place to start. If you don't have these, they are essential. If you do have them, but they are not authentic or serve more as wall decorations than as what matters, then you should begin there.

At Florida Hospital ten years ago, we were somewhere in between. We had all the pieces. The mission statement was real and authentic, but some of the other things were contrived or created top-down without definition, broad understanding, or acceptance. So we worked back through this process to gain buy-in.

The point I am trying to make is that painting on canvas is both art and science. There are some great directional markers and methods, to be sure, but often you will find yourself off the grid without a navigation system. You will, as the definition of "imagination" suggests, see something in your organization's collective mind that has not existed before. For this reason, give yourself permission to get it wrong sometimes, stay open, and aggressively seek feedback and listen. Then adjust as you learn. And repeat!

EMERGENCY! STAY CALM

Ten years ago, the seven emergency departments of the Florida Hospital system sucked (a technical medical term). Internally, we all knew it. You heard it when you met someone in the community and they learned you worked at Florida Hospital. They couldn't help themselves. They seemed compelled to tell you about their most recent experience. And it was seldom a good one.

It usually started with, "I waited." And too many times I would hear the voice in my head saying, "You're lucky, 'cause it's often much longer." You could feel it if you worked at Florida Hospital and needed an ED (Emergency Department), especially if you were a leader. Everyone learned to call ahead to someone you knew to expedite the process or take you in the side door to avoid the wait.

I found this difficult to accept. We had one system for executives and management and another for everyone else in the community. I understood it: we protect the ones we love and care about. I just didn't like it.

In the first months of my new role at Florida Hospital, I gathered the team to dialogue about what we needed to focus on. Where should we start the transformation? Where was the biggest bang for the buck?

I knew whatever we chose had to be clear and compelling. I suggested much would be made of this new leader and his team by what we did early in our journey together. It had to make sense to our twenty thousand employees and physicians without a wordy PowerPoint presentation. I suggested the ED. I told the team that I thought it was broken and had been for two decades. I boiled down the hospital business and operations to its simplest structure. The front door was the ED and the back door was our operating rooms. If we expected to grow and serve our community, both of those doors had to be open and inviting.

There is a little-understood process that often occurs in EDs across the nation. It's called *divert*. When you are reaching what you believe is capacity, you place a call to the ambulance companies and let them know you are no longer accepting patients. Another strange happening we experienced was the amount of what is called "left without being seen" cases. These are people who show up at the ED, check in, get tired of waiting, and leave.

I used an analogy that this is like going to a restaurant, getting drinks and a menu, and then leaving. It's awkward, to say the least. Most of us have to be pretty dissatisfied to actually do this. And yet we had 5 to 10 percent of our potential patients (customers) doing this every day. The word of mouth must be killing our brand. The lost revenue alone was more than disturbing. Worse, this had to be occasionally dangerous for those patients who left. It just wasn't acceptable.

I made a pitch to the team that the ED was what we first needed to fix. It mattered. It was the number-one thing board members complained about. It was the main story we heard from people in the community. Staff knew it was a problem. From a financial perspective, it would provide revenue, growth, and market share and reduce cost. It struck me as a win, win, win.

It caught me off guard when the strong pushback came. They weren't arguing that the ED didn't need fixing. They argued that it was too hard. The problem was that it had been attempted several times in the past by some of the best leaders in the company without much success. I wondered whom they didn't have confidence in: me, them, or us. In the listening and unpacking, it became clear they were mostly being protective. They were applying a very traditional and conventional axiom. They urged me to pick something that would give the team and me a small win to build some momentum.

But now, back to the earlier part of the chapter and the opportunity to paint a big, beautiful, and brilliant brushstroke across the canvas. I could not see a better place to begin to paint. If people thought it was too hard and we succeeded, they would know they could conquer anything. Two decades of failure and poor performance erased. Reluctantly, the team accepted that I probably wasn't going to back away from this challenge. We ventured forward, all oars in the water.

IF AT FIRST YOU DON'T SUCCEED, CONSIDER GIVING UP

In the beginning, we failed much more than we succeeded. We began to realize that the goal was too vague: fix the EDs. We had failed to set clear goals, and thus we had developed a habit of making "legitimate" excuses. We also had a knack for something I termed *complexification*. If simplicity were needed, we seemed bent on making it more complicated.

We went back to the drawing board with a question: What does a customer or patient want when they come to the ED? It took several meetings to get to an answer. We often got lost in our administrative and clinical perspectives, colored by regulations, clinical protocols, and resource requirements.

But after a series of childlike *why, why, why* questions, the answer finally emerged: "They want to see a doctor." That's it. After many months of failure and frustration, that was the big aha moment.

And what do they want *after* they have seen the doctor? "They want to go home, or they want a bed in the hospital if they are being admitted." Of course. Our work is done. Everything we do must be directed to that. "In the future, I don't want to know anything about the ED except the time from door to doctor," I stated. "And, after that, I want to know how long till the patient was able to return home or we had them comfortably in a hospital bed." This approach was affectionately named the 3 Ds: door to doctor, door to discharge (going home), and door to departure (being admitted). Every department in the hospital understood that if they had an effect on these 3 Ds, they had to have a plan to affect them positively.

I know people were shocked that I didn't want to know about the budget, the labor costs, volumes, patient-satisfaction scores, and a host of other metrics we had routinely focused on. For a former finance guy and someone who loves the data, it was unnatural behavior. But it was impossible for the staff with a patient in front of them to even think about a laundry basket of metrics. They needed a single, clear mission. We bet that the other metrics would improve if we painted on the canvas with clarity and helped people know what we really cared about. This proved true. Almost two years later, a finance manager presented me with one of the most creative and complex graphs I think I have ever seen. At least twelve performance metrics from the ED were on it. All the lines were intertwining and overlapping yet with one common characteristic: up and to the right, all consistently and significantly improving. Our assumption had been correct.

HARD LESSONS: LISTENING TO LEAD

I was starting to feel good about the team's early successes when the chief of emergency medicine, the physician responsible for the medical staff side of the operation, pulled me aside. Dr. Reagan Schwartz is one of the finest human beings I have ever worked with. He graciously explained to me that, if I would involve the physicians, they could help. They *wanted* to help. I was stunned.

I thought I had involved them more than we had engaged any group of physicians. I had not learned to ask for feedback consistently, and, worse, I had too eagerly accepted my own assumption that I was doing well leading these physicians. Lesson learned, at least until the next time I forgot that engagement is in the eye of the engaged, not the engager. Dr Schwartz was right: the physicians showed up huge, and you could feel another strong turn of the performance flywheel.

With this new turn, the first noticeable improvement came from our largest and most complex ED at our downtown campus. How could this be? I would have thought the first movement would have come from a smaller and less complex operation. Even more puzzling to me was the fact that the director of this unit was relatively new. She had just transferred from one of the smallest emergency departments where she had served as the assistant director.

This I had to understand. One afternoon, I walked across the street to the hospital ED and asked for the director, Trish Price. I wanted to see what an ED leader looked like who was moving the needle. I was directed to a back hallway. Once in the hallway, I followed the sound of voices to a storage closet. I stepped into the closet and said, "I am looking for Trish."

"I am Trish," came the energetic response in a Southern drawl.

She was in scrubs. Not the traditional attire for management. She also seemed young for this responsibility. But she was clearly making a difference. I was surprised by my internal reaction and the assumptions I was again making. I don't think you know where imagination will come from or what it looks like. Experience is important, but so is courage, heart, a roll-up-the-sleeves attitude, and a pair of scrubs. She was redefining the symbols of leadership and creating an environment of leading from the front, not the back. Just what we needed for the "front door" of the hospital, our ED.

Next came the tipping point in this journey, combined with an unforgettable lesson. Rob Fulbright, a talented and focused young leader, led our second-largest hospital. He stopped by my office with an idea. He wanted to advertise a sixty-minute guarantee to see a doctor. We were not even close to achieving this performance level. However, he reasoned that if we made this commitment, we would be forced to figure it out. I was intrigued, but mostly I was skeptical. Similar to my reaction to Trish, I thought, *I love his enthusiasm, but he is certainly naïve to the difficulty of doing this, not to mention the likely public embarrassment and customer dissatisfaction.* This was a real risk.

I listened, asked him a few questions, and told him I thought we should talk about it with the rest of the team. Whatever he deployed would affect the other hospital campuses, and the team needed to weigh in on his idea. The marketing team expressed concern about the strategy. We couldn't afford a black eye. At the time, we were early into breaking up the silos, and we were challenging our language of control, like "Stay in your lane." Rob was clearly out of his lane.

A few weeks later, Rob convinced us that he could execute this plan. So we labeled it a pilot and gave the green light. It worked for a couple months, and then it came apart. We pushed the pause button on the ads and analyzed what worked and what didn't. The conclusion was that we drove it too much from the top, didn't fully get buy-in from the staff and physicians, and did not gain the critical support needed from the radiology and lab departments along with the nursing floors. The innovation of an ED door-to-doctor guarantee, while common now, was very new to the industry at that time. It was a marketing success and volumes increased as a direct result. Our processes were not fully hardened to scale as more and more patients chose this ED.

Much credit is given to Rob and his team; they learned very quickly and, within a short time, were back in the hunt for a breakthrough. Sure enough, they not only got back to their earlier performance, but they also exceeded it. And then, to my delight, they sustained it. However, the breakthrough story was not over. This would come in a powerful mindset and culture shift from this team's process.

Every month, we had a focused review of results from our ED work. These reviews were a stroke on the canvas. They were set up to move away from habits that had quietly crept into our culture over the years. My training as an accountant had given me an idea how to expose it in a very definitive way: as a formula.

NONPERFORMANCE + GOOD STORY ≠ PERFORMANCE

I would write this on a whiteboard and then, with a bit of drama, draw a line through the equal-sign to make the point: nonperformance is always equal to nonperformance. These reviews became a time to share our performance and each leader's contribution with peers, partners, and teammates. They were designed with a "show me the data" section using a green, yellow, or red color palette to make clear the performance status. This was followed by sharing which strategies had worked to get your indicators to green and what your plan is for improving yellow and red results.

I still remember where I was sitting when Rob shared a comprehensive review of the sixty-minute guarantee and all they had done, all they had learned, and all that was now working. I watched a curious thing occur about halfway through his report. Dr. Monica Reed, who led our Celebration Health hospital campus located in the town of Celebration, turned around and began whispering to her team. She is a high innovator with natural leadership ability. But this was the first hospital she had ever run. And she was the first physician in our system to be given this responsibility.

This hospital was a showcase hospital as a result of its location next to and the relationship with Walt Disney World, and the unique mission with which it was endowed by Florida Hospital at its creation. Over the last decade, it had achieved some of those aims, but without consistent operating excellence (which it did not have), I felt those larger aims would be undermined. When we gave Monica this assignment, I shared very directly that we needed her to run a great hospital *and* achieve the rest of the higher aims for this special place. I knew she felt this burden, and its pressures weighed on her.

The whispering continued. Fortunately, I was quickly developing a skill to observe the team and had a knack for catching a good bit of the words they would occasionally and quietly share with the person next to them during a meeting. Monica was directing them to figure out how to apply the learnings Rob was articulating to the challenges at Celebration.

Prior to this, there was a dysfunctional competition among the hospitals. It expressed itself in secretive work and a lack of sharing and collaboration along the way. We were individual teams competing for the prize instead of one team working together. It looked more like the NCAA basketball tournament than a health system serving patients at *all* our emergency rooms. It was indeed one mission and one brand. These two executives struck the deathblow to this competition. We would only get better together.

The second friction affecting the speed of our flywheel was ownership. This was still the COO's priority. People cared, to be sure, but there was a long legacy of top-down leading and the notion of what does "administration" want. At the same instance of Monica's whispering, the transfer of ownership had occurred between hospital leadership and me, for the performance and ownership of their EDs and the rest of operations, and eventually for the organization's strategy. They no longer saw performance of the EDs as my project, my push, my cajoling, or my commitment, but they saw it as their project, their patients, and, ultimately, their fulfillment of the mission. This became a beautiful (perhaps a vivid purple-and-blue) brushstroke on the canvas. This, along with a hundred other smaller things, consistently done over that year continued to accelerate through the next seven years. We never lost sight of our front door. Indeed, it transformed us.

WHEN DISNEY IS YOUR PARTNER

We benefited from a gift that came in two forms. The first was having one of the world's most-recognized brands for understanding and creating culture as our partner. The folks at Disney are masters at painting the canvas. This gave us the inspiration to learn and proximity to observe them up close.

The second gift came in the form of a person. His name is Al Weiss, the CEO of Walt Disney World Parks. Des Cummings, our executive vice president for business development, and Marla Silliman, who led the children's services departments, were eating breakfast with Al when he said, "Let's think big." That conversation led to the creation of Florida Hospital for Children at the Disney Pavilion.

We received a very generous financial gift and a lobby designed and built by the Disney Imagineers in the renovated space that was to become the children's hospital. These gifts alone were incredible. The lobby these professional "imaginers" created was one of my regular and favorite stops as I rounded throughout the hospital. But that was only a small part of the gifts they gave us.

The more significant gift was a challenge, along with their insight, know-how, and passion to imagine and create a culture of customer service. The date was set for the joint announcement of this first-in-the-nation partnership between Disney and a children's hospital. I was enamored with the Disney mystique. Growing up, I loved Sunday nights at 7 p.m., when *The Wonderful World of Disney* aired. The decision to move to Orlando and accept a job at Florida Hospital was partly influenced by its proximity to Disney.

The day arrived for the press conference. It was overcast with a light rain. I began to joke that it never rained on a major Disney production. I knew they had control of all the elements. But as I watched Marla, Al, Des, and others take the stage escorted by Mickey and Minnie with a very happy playlist blasting through the speakers, a seriousness took hold of me. Disney was one of the world's leading brands. They were taking a risk to allow their brand next to ours. We had a limited track record in providing children's care. How were we going to turn this into a full-service children's hospital *and* do it in a way that did not diminish the Disney brand? I felt a cold sweat that was not from the continued rain.

The event concluded. Mickey and Minnie left, along with most of the crowd. All that was left were a few lingerers who just wanted to take it all in. I found Marla. I congratulated her on this milestone. Next I asked, "Do you understand what changed today?" I didn't wait for her answer. I had been absorbing the answer to this question through the entire ceremony. I blurted out, "Everything."

She nodded her head, letting me know she had already grasped the full meaning. She knew she now had to deliver the extraordinary—and do it on budget, on time, with an experience and clinical excellence worthy of the Disney Pavilion. She did, along with her team.

However, we had help. You may not know this but Disney also runs the Disney Institute, at which they train companies and organizations from all over the world in customer service. This division is led by my friend, encourager, and hyper-imaginative thinker and doer, Jeff James.

The first thing they taught us about customer service is that it's mostly about culture. We learned that getting our processes oriented to serve our team members was one of our first jobs as leaders. We had to know what our team needed to succeed with our customers or patients. We were daily challenged with how hard many of our processes made it for our nurses and staff to serve and love well.

One of my favorite statements from our training was, "It's not magical. It's methodical." There is a passage in Scripture that states, "a little child shall lead them" (Isaiah 11:6). So the work with the Disney Institute was focused on preparing our new "Florida Hospital for Children," but that work soon spilled over to our adult services and the entire hospital. We took that methodical mindset to heart in the detail-process work that led to our ISO 9001 quality certification, but also in the work of creating the culture of teamwork that would sustain us in our quest.

There is a wonderful story from the very beginning of Disney as a company and the power of creating the environment. "Walt adored the teamwork at his growing studio. Just as in Marceline (Missouri, where Walt was from), where farmers worked together building fences, harvesting the fields, and killing hogs, animation was, by its nature, a community activity. Everyone contributed gags and story ideas. The top animators drew hundreds of key scenes for a picture and the underlings— some of whom were appropriately called in-betweeners—filled in the many drawings that connected them. Putting music and art together required close collaboration and patience. In Walt's view there were no stars in this universe, only team members working together to make each picture better than the last."

This is a story from the early days of Disney but also the story of creating culture, supported by the environment required to lead with imagination.

IN THE END

There are both subtle and not-so-subtle ways we can mar the canvas. A poorly communicated change in employee benefits. An attempt, whether written or publicly spoken, to deliver difficult news, but diligently working to spin it positively. It's a trust-killer and doesn't really work (most people see right through it). The approach of "people can't handle the truth" didn't work for Jack Nicholson in the movie *A Few Good Men*, and it doesn't work in organizations that want a vibrant, creative, and performance-based culture.

It often occurs without negative intent but rather from the velocity and pace of change we all deal with. It also happens because of our desire to "get stuff done." However, people want to be involved in work that matters and has purpose. This means they want to know the thinking and the direction of their leaders. They are investing themselves in the efforts. They want to feel successful, and they want their opinions to matter. If they believe their efforts are making a difference, they will invest more. This is a win, win, win. You and the company win, your people win, and the customer wins.

When we start seeing the environment as culture, culture as people, and people as people we love, imagination comes alive. It influences the thinking of your team. As the environment becomes increasingly consistent, it allows action to flow from that thinking, and that action translates into love for the people you serve. Regularly, visitors and guests would ask me, "How do you get all your people to be so nice?" This was often followed by a story of an event they had experienced. It was how these visitors were made to feel in their interactions that was at the root of their question.

So much of the work to design and develop culture is proactive, creative, and, yes, once in a while it's about showing up and being present. However, there is a part of this work that involves challenging our traditions and assumptions. Sometimes it looks like taking a stand, but other times it might be a redirect. The following story contains both elements.

The problem was that our sponsor organization was out of space, and they decided to build a new corporate headquarters. The architects began their work with a series of interviews to determine "programmatic" needs. Boil it down and that means who gets what locations, who gets what size and type of office (corner with a window, anyone?), and how will it be furnished and decorated.

Our Florida Hospital building was also old, and our team was scattered in several other buildings. It was decided that a new state of Florida headquarters would be built. The same architects were chosen to keep these two projects in sync. As we met with the architects to begin the process to determine the "programmatic" needs, they shared that at the corporate office it had been made clear they ran it as a "meritocracy." This meant the senior leaders had earned the right to occupy the best space, meaning the top floor. The largest offices and the best furnishings to go with the top floor.

Many of the Florida Hospital senior executives were in attendance, and I could feel their gaze turning toward me. The unspoken message was clear: Are we following the same path in this building? It doesn't really fit with our culture of "the best idea wins," does it? I then turned my gaze to the Division CEO who was leading the project. He astutely read the group's body language and my expression. In as politically correct manner as he could, he shared with the architect that, while there is "nothing wrong" with that approach, it probably wouldn't work here.

I had already been considering where the Florida Hospital executive team would be housed. I did not want to continue the stereotype or tradition of the senior executive offices on the top floor. It put them farthest away from the staff, doctors, and patients. Our largest campus had this legacy built in, and I watched the way it affected the language, thinking, and perceptions of everybody, including the executives and administrative assistants who inhabited this "top" floor.

Yet we struggled with who we could put on that top floor. There is so much symbolism in this decision. I thought about our fundraising group, but then the caregivers might think we thought that was more important than taking care of patients. Perhaps the clinical team. But that might communicate only direct caregivers matter and not the thousands who make it possible for them to do their work effectively. You can quickly see the rabbit holes in each choice we considered.

One night, I shared our dilemma and the various considerations that were underway with my wife. She cut through my haze in only a matter of minutes. "Why don't you make the top floor flexible workspace, your boardroom, and do it creatively to support the concepts of teamwork and collaboration you are always talking about." She even played with the notion that, when we had a tough problem, people might say, "Let's take it to eight," the top floor. This could be a physical message of "the best idea wins" and further harden our commitment to our culture.

The next day, we decided to do exactly that. People noticed. Several months after it opened, I was sitting in the lobby space that opened out from the boardroom and several of the flexible workrooms. We had designed it with a common area and a buffet to cater meals. A group of physicians was meeting in a leadership development class. Directors developing a customer-service strategy were in the large flex space. Senior clinical leaders were in the back room struggling to understand some new data we had received on our clinical outcomes.

Suddenly, it was noisy—the good kind—full of energy and possibility. It was lunchtime. All three groups were gathering in line together, potluck-style, dishing out their meals. This was exactly what we had imagined two years earlier in the design of the building and space. It was one picture of many. People were painting on the canvas of who and what we were striving to be. This space belonged to everyone who was contributing to our success. The power of the many was being released.

The stage was set.

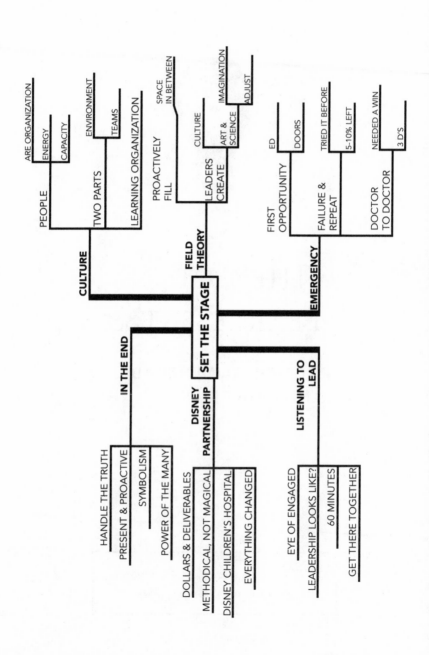

The Act of Fearlessness

PRACTICING VULNERABILITY AND RIGHT RISK-TAKING

"Go out on a limb, that is where the fruit is." —*Jimmy Carter*

LEADERSHIP LYRIC

CREATIVE CONCEPT: SYNCHRONICITY

Synchronicity is the notion of things being connected without seeming causal. Translated to the stage, synchronicity occurs as a performer's entrance is coordinated with props, lighting, bandmember placements, costumes or clothing, stage personas, and a host of other things that create the performance and action.

SUMMARY

Vulnerability is about putting yourself in harm's potential way, or "out there," in order to accomplish something. It requires clear and creative action. It exposes you. In that place of exposure, we move from preparing to lead to leading with imagination. First, we take risks personally, then we can begin taking right risks organizationally. This is where the trifecta of imagination, creativity, and innovation get their solid foothold in what might be described as virtuous momentum.

WHAT MAKES US EAGER TO BE VULNERABLE?

Actually, I don't know if I have ever met anyone eager to be vulnerable. I have met a few people who I thought took crazy physical risks. To me, that seemed more like an addiction to adrenaline and thrill-seeking, than risk-taking. That isn't what I'm talking about. Nor am I talking about the bold business risk-taking of an ego-driven CEO who recklessly bets his company. Sometimes they bet correctly, and the media extols these people.

No, the vulnerability and risk-taking I'm talking about is the kind that requires you to put yourself, your ideas, and your creations *out there*—where others may criticize, chastise, and cast aside a part of you. There is something deep in humanness that seeks to avoid these places, as well as something in all of us that, sadly, at times participates in doing this to others.

You can probably recall an incident from your childhood that still affects you. Two events quickly come to mind for me. As a child, I had thick hair with a slight curl to it. I liked it on the longish side, and sometimes my friends called me "Brillo Pad" as a result of its texture and look. That was okay and resulted in only mild trauma. The real trauma came when my parents occasionally demanded a haircut. I would have preferred a minor trim. But spending money to leave most of my hair still attached did not make sense to them. A full cut was all that would do.

The resulting change from "Brillo Pad" to baldy always got a slew of commentary, including my favorite, "Did you run into a lawnmower?" I would stress out for days leading up to the haircut. Heading to the school bus the next day, I would fight the urge to run back home and stay there until my hair grew back. I dreaded the impending teases and taunts of my classmates. It was real then and still is now (a little) as I relive it.

If we all spent a few hours together, I am sure we could fill a book with examples of how each one of us learned to avoid these situations that made us feel exposed and vulnerable. Fitting in becomes more important than finding our unique voice or place. That feeling is difficult to overcome, even as adults. This leftover from our childhood diminishes our ability to access imagination and to act upon it.

PUSHING THE POLE

The willingness to be vulnerable starts with answering *yes* to a question. Early in my tenure as COO, I received an insistent call from Tony Dottino, a consultant the hospital had hired to engage nurses on the front lines. Tony had developed a program called "Grassroots." He shared that he was conducting a workshop with about seventy-five nurses at the hospital. They were very upset, saying nobody "at the top" was listening. He asked if I would be willing to listen to their concerns. My instinct was to say *no*. I thought, *There must be someone more appropriate than me to handle this request, like the chief nursing officer, or anyone else, for that matter.*

But one of the basic ingredients of choosing to be vulnerable is a bit of courage. In my case, sometimes it helps me to act before I overthink (and think about those feelings after my haircuts). I responded with a resigned, "Yes. Where are you meeting?" I grabbed my suit coat and walked out of my office toward the basement of the hospital—my unplanned destination. I turned around and walked back to my office. My assistant shot a smile my way. It wasn't the first time I had forgotten something and had to return to the office. I looked back at her as I removed my jacket, hung it back up, and again headed down the hallway to the elevator. I am sure she was wondering what that was all about.

Suit jackets can sometimes double as battle gear to project power and control. But I had already learned that listening is not about control; it is about openness. A suit jacket would have sent an immediate signal to the group of employees in the room about what was getting ready to happen. I was already a "suit" to these nurses, already the owner of multiple strikes against me walking into the room. Taking the jacket off wouldn't get me back to break-even in the strike count, but it was at least a small gesture of my willingness to be with them.

When I arrived, they were deep in a table exercise and discussion. I picked a table, sat down, and listened in. I think I even made a comment or two. I am sure they wondered why I was crashing their group, but I am also sure they had no idea who I was. A few minutes later, Tony called their attention back to the front. He shared with the group that he had taken a risk, called the new COO, and asked if I would come over to hear their concerns. He told them I had said yes, that he thought that was a start, and he hoped they would say to me what they had said to him. With little additional fanfare, he introduced me and sat down.

And share they did—at first intensely and tinged with anger. Gradually, the intensity lessened and turned to a genuine concern for their ability to care for their patients. It culminated in a request and a profound moment. They asked if I would be willing to "push the pole," an IV pole. If you've ever been a patient in a hospital, you understand. If you have visited a hospital, you likely understand. They are supposed to roll easily and allow you to move with bags of necessary medication slowly dripping into your body through an intravenous line.

Apparently, at Florida Hospital, the vast majority of the IV poles did not function correctly. This created a problem for patients, nurses, and transporters. And now, for one very out-of-touch executive. I agreed to their request and tried to push the pole. It looked new enough to me, but it surely did not roll. I tried multiple times to find the trick to cause "rollation." Failing in front of this audience, feeling a little flush coming over me, I just picked it up and moved it. They roared with laughter and then broke into unexpected applause. When the roar died, the humor was beginning to find its mark with me as well. I acknowledged the failure, apologized for the organization's processes that had allowed this situation to go unresolved, and asked what they needed to address the most urgent cases.

As the meeting dismissed, I found myself surrounded by caring and talkative nurses thanking me for coming, apologizing if they had caused offense, and eager to talk about their passion for serving their patients and the organization better. I walked out changed. The fear I had going in was real. But the reward far outweighed the risk. I felt good. And I think they were hopeful for the future.

In *The Advantage: Why Organizational Health Trumps Everything Else in Business*, Patrick Lencioni makes a compelling point about employees: "It is not so much an intellectual process as an emotional one." Pushing the pole created an emotional connection, born out of a willingness to be vulnerable.

Sometimes the risks (as in this case) are pretty low. But other times they are not. And the consequences are very real for you and the organization. Sometimes they will require you to face deep insecurities and entrenched assumptions about yourself. This is the next level of personal vulnerability.

WHAT IT MEANS TO GO DEEPER

In the months leading up to my transition from being the financial officer to becoming the operating officer, the organization was in the process of preparing for our Joint Commission accreditation. This is the license to be a hospital and remain a provider for all government programs, like Medicare and Medicaid, as well as with most insurance companies. In other words, accreditation is very, very important.

At that time, the Joint Commission was changing the way they surveyed hospitals by moving from a document and policy review to a "tracer" methodology. This new approach evaluated the actual care of patients through their entire stay in the hospital. Logically, this is a beneficial change to assure hospitals are caring for patients in a safe and effective way. But this was new for them and for us, which gave us reasonable concern.

I began asking questions prior to the transition about our understanding of the new process and our preparedness. Everyone involved seemed quite confident. I certainly did not have a background to question them, so I took it at face value. We had never had an issue before, and the vast majority of hospitals in the country certainly passed, so it seemed a fairly minor risk. Besides, what would the government and insurers do if we were not able to care for their patients? Our competitor did not have the capacity to treat all the people who would need care.

Only a few months after I was installed as the COO, the Joint Commission arrived unannounced to survey our hospital. They brought ten surveyors with a plan to roam our seven hospital campuses for five days looking for problems. The new survey process allowed a maximum of eleven citations (problems) before a hospital lost its full accreditation. Eleven to seventeen citations earned a hospital a provisional status, and more than seventeen was a fail. Their model, however, did not adjust for a hospital's size. You were either over 105 beds or under. We had over two thousand beds. This created a rich environment to find eleven issues given the vast numbers of patients and processes we took care of.

After day one, things seemed to be going pretty well, helping to calm my earlier concerns. Then day two came along. Most of the day went well, except for one minor incident in what is called a neuro-interventional lab. It's like an operating room, where they put a coil- or catheter-like instrument into your brain to treat blockages or relieve an aneurysm. It is often a lifesaving procedure, and we had one of the most skilled physicians in the region on our staff.

In an operating or procedural room, there is a process every hospital is required to do called "pause for the cause." This is a double check for the physician and team to make sure they have the correct patient, the correct procedure, the correct body part, and the correct side (laterality) of your body. However, in some areas, it becomes a bit overkill to the clinicians, especially in places like the neuro-interventional lab because there is only one brain, and the patient generally arrives with an acute need that is well understood prior to arrival. With these procedures, time is of the essence. But the Joint Commission (understandably so) does not have a good way of distinguishing the types of environments this process works well for and which ones it does not. So, all surgical environments are required to follow this process.

In any event, a team of surveyors was observing a case in this particular lab. Music was loudly playing in the room (something many surgeons do), and a wall was partially blocking the surveyors' observations. A case came in and proceeded. The surveyors did not observe a pause and recorded this. Later they checked the records and saw that the staff had documented a pause. This troubled the surveyors—as it should have. I was notified of the issue. Along with the notification was an indication that the surveyors might consider suspending the entire survey as a result of this one issue.

I was confused about why this might be the case. We all took this concern very seriously and soon learned that the surveyors believed there was a falsification of the record—a very bad thing, to be sure. I immediately directed that the two staff members be summoned to a conference room and insisted that no one was to explain or question them prior to their arrival. Once they arrived, together with the surveyors, we asked them about the case in question and what occurred. They explained, and everything seemed to be in order. As the patient was wheeled in, they were located behind the wall where they had performed the pause for the cause. The music was loud, so the surveyors likely could not hear, and the wall created an obstruction. Both staff members maintained the same story, along with the physician.

We dismissed the staff. The lead surveyor told us they would report on this in the morning after discussion among their team. I left feeling comfortable both with our handling of the concern and the outcome. We could not be accused of co-opting the staff's story. The surveyors heard the same story we did, and I thought it was a very logical explanation. But sometimes things don't go the way you think they should.

The next morning, the physician surveyor who led the team assigned to the neuro lab said he was distressed to share their conclusion of a falsification of the record. They would be suspending the survey. This essentially meant that we'd failed. *Now what?*

The head of the survey team, who was sitting next to me, explained our rights. We had the right to appeal, and she described the process to do so. She also shared that we may still be in jepearody as a result of the violations we were accumulating. I stated that we would be appealing, so let's start that right away. This just couldn't happen.

Later that day, we received word from Joint Commission headquarters in Chicago that our appeal had resulted in our suspension being overturned and our survey would continue. Disaster averted. Thursday, day four, was a quiet one, which bolstered our confidence that we had likely and perhaps skillfully managed our way through a very challenging and never-before-encountered situation with the accreditation process.

After a long and difficult week, day five arrived. We sat down in a large conference room at 2:00 p.m. for the closing meeting.

These events always produce a mixed set of emotions. The draining of adrenaline from an intense process, much like the release of finishing a difficult exam, was palpable. Yet so was the uncertainty as we prepared to hear the preliminary report from the survey team. The room was packed full of executives, the clinical team that had managed the day-to-day of the survey, and the ten surveyors. Because of our size and the lack of a large-enough space, we also had a group of probably forty additional staff from the quality and accreditation team on a phone conference line. They were the ones who had been in early and had left late each day supporting the survey process. They were an all-in, fully engaged group of people.

It took less than ten minutes for the lead surveyor to convey that we had twenty-nine deficiencies against the eleven we were allowed to have in order to earn full accreditation. Panic and shock set in. My mind raced, first to my situation: the former CFO turned COO. In an instant, I imagined (a wrong way to use imagination, by the way) the headline in the paper the next day: "Florida Hospital Taps CFO to Lead. They Fail the Joint Commission." Oh yeah, and a subheading, *Let that be a lesson to all of you.*

Next I went to the implications for the hospital as well as for our sponsor, Adventist Health System. What would happen when the world discovered their flagship hospital had failed accreditation? Then, someone tapped me on the shoulder and asked if I wanted to kill the conference call phone line. My mind still racing, I responded *yes.* After all, we didn't know who else might be on the line. For heaven's sake, there might be a reporter on already. The rest of the meeting and day were a blur.

We began to chart a path through this unfamiliar crisis. Of the many communications that afternoon and into the evening, two stood out. The first was a call to Dr. David Moorhead at Loma Linda University Medical Center, outside Los Angeles. He had just agreed to join our team, as the chief medical officer, but was not scheduled to arrive for another month. With the calm and confidence of the gifted surgeon he is, he said something like, "This is not good. I will be on a plane Sunday, and we can meet first thing Monday morning." I was so grateful for his decisive leadership and his employer's generosity in allowing him to come and help.

The second was an email from Dr. Lee Adler, which arrived in my inbox just before sundown. Dr. Adler was responsible for the team working directly with the surveyors, so I decided to open it before ending my workday.

In his straightforward way, he described his disappointment at my closing the phone lines down and the message it sent to his people. He shared that the team felt disrespected and diminished. I was furious, first with his timing and obvious lack of understanding about the gravity of our situation. I was also furious with his smallminded staff who were putting their feelings ahead of the real issues. I know this doesn't sound pretty or politically correct, but that is the unvarnished truth. I keep a sunset to sunset Sabbath. I am convinced that had I not, the next part of this story would have been very different. But because I was exhausted and the sun was already setting, and mostly out of habit, I closed the computer. I decided I would respond with both barrels Sunday when I had a good bit more energy to express myself.

Sunday morning, as I opened my computer, my failed attempt to "push the pole" came into view. I reminded myself to listen to what this group of people were telling me. I replayed *all* the events of the last week and took a hard look at my performance. Then it hit me. They were *right*. The email I wrote in response was a simple one: "Please assemble the team of people that I affected as soon as feasible. I would like to talk with them in person." I walked the short distance from my office, across the railroad tracks, around the corner, and into the large, open workspace.

My thought process went something like this: I'd failed to lead and to be the leader they deserved. I could try to hide that—maybe I should do that. I had seldom seen leaders get up and admit this kind of failure. But something compelled me. I knew there were many who were not happy when I had been appointed to this role. I had no track record in operations, and I disrupted some other well-deserving executives' career paths. Worst case, I would likely be asked to resign. Someone has to take the blame when you fail the Joint Commission accreditation. Best case, I would be exposed, and the people I was supposed to lead would lose confidence in me. I once saw a bumper sticker that read, "The Struggle Is Real." That sums up what I felt as I walked into the meeting.

I greeted Dr. Adler and stepped into the room. I was immediately overwhelmed by the number of people. It wasn't the forty I expected, but close to one hundred. *Great, the grapevine will be working overtime to broadcast the massive crash-and-burn about to happen.* I suddenly felt emotion welling up in me. I had to compose my voice, then began saying something like this: "Dr. Adler sent me an email late Friday telling me of his and your distress with my actions earlier in the day. When I read it, I was *pissed*."

I continued, "I was angry at him and you for not understanding the choice I thought I had to make to protect the organization." The room was silent. I am not sure they had ever had an executive speak this bluntly and honestly about their feelings. And I am sure they wondered what was coming next. (In truth, I was kind of wondering what was coming next myself.)

"But on Sunday morning, when I began thinking about my email response, I realized something that stopped me cold. I had failed myself, the organization, and each of you. I wanted to come here today to tell you that personally. I want to affirm Dr. Adler for trusting me enough to tell me his truth and yours, hopefully with a sense there would not be retribution for it. Now, I want you to know how sorry I am for not being the leader you have a right to expect. I knew on Wednesday that we might fail. I managed to convince myself that it couldn't really happen.

"Even with that belief, I should have anticipated the possibility and had a plan B, just in case. You had a right to expect that, not a panicked leader reacting to the stimulus presented to him. I am sorry for making you feel devalued, for my lack of planning, and I hope to learn from this mistake."

At that point, I was barely holding on to my emotions—another vulnerability I was still learning to allow. I quickly excused myself and made the trek back across the railroad tracks to my office. I sat quietly, wondering what would come next. To my surprise, I began receiving emails almost instantly: "Thank you for sharing. It was incredibly meaningful." "We will follow you anywhere. We know we can trust you to not persist a course out of your ego and need to be right. We all failed and you demonstrated it was safe to admit that and then work to correct the mistake."

Somewhere on my journey back across the railroad tracks, I experienced freedom. An important book makes the statement that "the truth will set you free." As I reflected on the feedback that came so quickly and convincingly, another truth emerged: in the freedom of acting to be vulnerable, the organization began to be free and it opened a space and place for imagination to take root.

WHAT IT MEANS TO GO BIGGER

At the next level, the risk goes up both for you and the organization. But this is where payoffs usually live. Building capability or engaging in training doesn't translate to a business gain unless you take actions and ultimately lead your team or company to take real leaps or steps forward. In 2008, the federal government approved a new accrediting organization for the first time in over forty years. This provided an alternative to accreditation from the Joint Commission.

When we learned of this option, I asked our team to study it and make a recommendation. I know what many of you are probably thinking: we were upset with the Joint Commission for the last survey and wanted to avoid them in the next round. We eventually received full accreditation thanks to Dr. Moorhead and especially to a talented executive named Lee Johnson. She oversaw an intense process to prove our performance by statistical sampling to demonstrate the shortcomings of the new process applied to a large setting like ours. We also went through an additional survey three years later in the normal cycle and passed with flying colors.

It would have been much easier to continue in the known ways and with the current functioning systems. But we had a problem. For years we had used the pressure of the Joint Commission to cajole and corral our doctors into following the rules required by them. I had used a phrase often that these requirements were a "proxy for safety" in our hospital. But with so much progress behind us in this arena, it was no longer a statement that the team nor I felt we could continue to say with integrity. This was the impetus for exploring an alternative: the *Det Norske Veritas* (DNV), which translates to "the Norwegian truth." I live under an assumption that I am part Norwegian based on a story from my grandmother. The Norwegian truth sounded quite right!

This organization's history came out of the late 1800s and the shipbuilding industry. It was the heyday of shipping and shipbuilding. But there was one problem: too many ships were sinking. So Lloyd's of London, the insurer whose policies covered many of these ships, helped found the DNV to create and monitor standards of quality and processes to improve the building of ships. Today they use a system called ISO, which has been adopted in industries from jet-engine makers to oil-rig operators (including my friends Tim and Marie Kuck at Regal Marine in Orlando, who build powerboats). It is strenuous and takes over three years to achieve this standard—a long time for someone as generally impatient as I am. And what happens if we don't achieve it and we have no way to be accredited?

The team completed their study and recommendations in a few months. I watched with some amusement as they moved from high skepticism to mild positivity, and, eventually, to a strong (and courageous) recommendation. Dr. Dave Moorhead, who led the process, and I walked through the factors weighing on us to accept the team's view. First, the stuff in the fear category, the places where I could feel the familiar dread of showing up to class after my haircut and preparing for a dose of humiliation and embarrassment. Deep breath.

The questions came in a flood. What would people say about leaving the Joint Commission? Were we leaving because we had a problem and were afraid of failing the Joint Commission again? What would our board and corporate office say? Would they even let us, or would they throw us out for even suggesting such a new adventure? What would the community's perception be? Would our competitor take advantage as a result and foster a story about why we were switching (knowing full well our primary competitor is comprised of very honorable and good people)? Would the insurance companies try to cancel or renegotiate contracts? And what would happen if we were not able to be process-focused across our now eight campuses and hundreds of nursing and clinical units? *What would failure even look like?*

Not to mention, how would the healthcare community and the Joint Commission respond? The Joint Commission is a very powerful organization, and this decision to jump ship was akin to telling your father you won't be following his rules anymore. Perhaps the most burning questions for me were: What will our doctors say, and will they use this to lessen their engagement in our journey to improve quality and safety?

Time to take another breath. As I am sure you noticed, the fears take over, just like when we take risks in our personal lives. I think most of you reading immediately related to these types of questions based on decisions you have faced. It is easy to fear the worst and more difficult to imagine the possibilities.

We eventually found our way to a plan that defined this new phase in our organization's history. I have five kids today, ranging from sixteen to thirty-one years of age. My wife deserves most of the credit for any success we've had in raising them. One of the things I observed was her process for rule-setting early in our kids' lives, then as teenagers, and then as college students and beyond. Early on, the rules are clear, rather arbitrary, and often for the good of the whole family operation. For example, bedtime may be at 9 p.m. so they are rested and ready for the next day, and Mom and Dad have a little quiet time. We didn't offer a lot of choices or discuss all the merits of the rule or why they existed in the first place. Then for their teenage years, there is some discussion and more flexibility.

Then they go off to college, and they tell you stories about how late they are out. The intemperance of it all. For an early riser like myself, this was sometimes almost more than I could take. But gradually, they began to adjust their schedule (often with Mom's coaching) because it did not align with their bigger aims and goals. They were making these choices for reasons that propelled their dreams and aspirations. Maturation is really an marvelous thing to watch. The process moves from *you* to *them*. You are no longer the creator and enforcer of the rules.

We used this metaphor to work past our fears of leaving the Joint Commission and saw that this was our time to grow up as an organization. It was a choice to learn to trust our physicians more and invest in their leadership, thereby creating space for them to be completely on board with the transition. It was a chance to fully live out our aspiration of building love into all interactions and giving the door to our imagination a strong kick open.

We made the decision and gained the support of our board and sponsor. We bought plane tickets to Chicago to visit the headquarters of the Joint Commission. Our group calmly explained our decision, gave a clear rationale, and acknowledged the tremendous work the Joint Commission had done and the thorough agenda for improvements they had created for us. Most importantly, we made certain they understood our decision was not punitive. They were nothing but gracious. They expressed deep appreciation for making the trip to share our decision in person and left the door open to return in the future if things didn't work out.

The decision to take direct control of our quality and safety destiny was, in retrospect, more significant than I think any of us realized. I believe it was a rocket booster to the results described in chapter 1. It further forced us to imagine what we really wanted to become and to build the disciplines and processes to move us there. There was no map for this next phase of work, and a GPS was of little use. But it began with building the willingness to be vulnerable at the personal level, and then at the organizational level, followed by taking action.

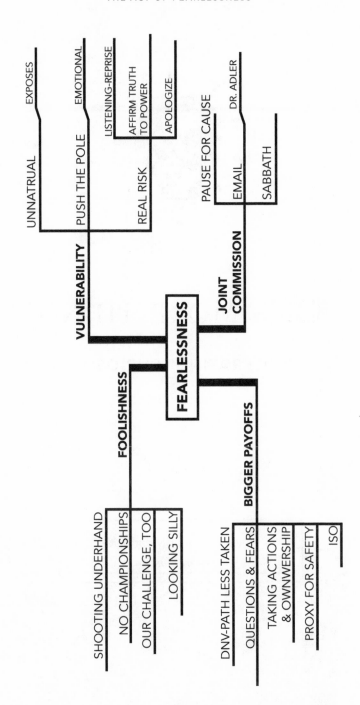

One More Thing

"TOLERATING" CURIOSITY

> "Never lose a holy curiosity."
> —*Albert Einstein*

LEADERSHIP LYRIC

CREATIVE CONCEPT: HISTORICAL FICTION

The historical novel requires a tension between facts and research that is truthful, and the creative activity of the investigator's imagination. It is understanding well what is known, while wondering and wandering into what is not known.

SUMMARY

Curiosity starts with questions. Both quality and quantity matter. Asking them is less than half the process. Holding the answer open, suspending judgment, questioning: do we even have the right question yet? That is the larger half. That is the art.

Curiosity is next about pursuing this process within the team, designing the space both physically and psychologically that is safe and collaborative, and tolerating the possible inefficiency of a "best idea wins" mind-set. It is being curious about customers and stakeholders, anchored with empathy. Far too many times, we stop asking *and* listening, believing we know the answers and leaving the most important insights undiscovered.

Finally, curiosity is about being relentless
and disciplined about the process.

DRUCKER REVISITED

Every organization needs a Des. What is a Des, you ask? A Des is a disruptor, someone willing to challenge conventional wisdom, willing to dream beyond next quarter's budget and financial targets, and willing to ask the questions that often elicit groans from the team. He is often "beyond Z," or down a different track altogether, and far ahead of what the rest of us were thinking.

Des Cummings served as executive vice president for mission and business development; he also played a key role in attracting me to the vision and possibility of Florida Hospital and as a mentor. He is a marketer and strategist at heart, in the best sense. A master storyteller and connector. Des gets the most meaningful parts of our being. And he understands the power and possibility of love.

Des played a key role in facilitating our development and understanding of the usefulness of curiosity. He painted on the canvas of culture that moved us to increasingly take risks and innovate in meaningful and productive ways. Curiosity, when done relentlessly, is hard work. Often, as Des was in "that mode," I would, at times, look at him and say, "You're making my head hurt."

He would just smile and most of the time, take a short pause to let me attempt to catch up before continuing. There were probably hundreds of idea seeds, innovations, or critical adaptions that were initiated by this process.

So, what does this have to do with Drucker? You may remember from chapter 1 this statement: "The only legitimate business functions were marketing and innovation." Des understood both and increasingly opened my eyes to the elegant and broad power in this idea to fuel the organization. Growing is all about asking what the customer is needing or wanting, and listening for the answer. The process of innovating and making the product better follows the same pattern, though more often applied to the team delivering or producing it.

WHEN I SPOKE AS A CHILD

Children understand the rudiments of curiosity. They are also uninhibited about the whole thing. I remember each of our children when they reached the age of four, and the quantity of questions they would ask, many starting with *why*. In later life, I have come to appreciate the power of a question that starts with why. Its effectiveness is undeniable.

Russell Ackoff, a pioneer of systems theory applied to management and a professor at the Wharton School, describes it like this: "Children up to about preschool age don't even know what constraints are; they don't make assumptions that dictate their behavior." He continues to describe the educational process: "Teachers (and parents) present problems and questions to children from the beginning of their schooling until its end. For each question or problem they present with few exceptions, they have an acceptable answer. To achieve academic success, students at all levels must learn how to provide those in positions of authority with the answers they expect. An answer they do not expect, however right or creative it might be, is considered wrong."

Unfortunately, and much too often, organizations continue this process. Education fosters this desire for conformity, while, as leaders, we place value on and reward compliance. Fortunately, we have the power to reengage our curiosity with clarity and competence. This is essential to leading with imagination. We must not simply tolerate but actively cultivate curiosity within the culture.

Curiosity played two roles for us at Florida Hospital. First, it helped us perform better as a team. Why? Because it facilitated a creative tension within our diverse team. This diversity was by design. As we set about to leverage curiosity in a "best idea wins" environment, we determined we had to ask better questions. We forced ourselves to learn to ask open-ended questions to understand each of the teams' perspectives. It took a few wins to reinforce the power this gave us, but, gradually, we began to appreciate our diversity more than be annoyed by it, and more importantly, we grew to appreciate its role in our decision-making.

We routinely questioned our process of curiosity in practice because it doesn't always look efficient in the present. This is one part of the art of leadership, and my experience is that you almost never get it quite right. What you can do is keep testing and shoot for "directionally correct." After every leadership conference with our top five hundred leaders, we would go through a simple set of questions: What went well? What could be improved? What is one thing we should do differently next time?

These meetings were tough, at least on me. I tended to get defensive. This desire to defend worked counterintuitively as well. The more trust we developed as a team, the more honest and brutal the feedback—and the stronger the urge to get defensive. I would most keenly feel it for the leaders responsible for planning these events, and, yes, they usually included me.

In almost all of these debriefs, someone would comment, "You asked the question, so this is my feedback, but please remember, I started by saying, 'I think this was the best meeting we have ever had.' " Yes, and thank you. It was so easy to forget that in the midst of feedback. It struck me that this was part of the work of moving from good to great. This was the discipline of the twenty-mile march Jim Collins talks about in his book of the same name (*Great by Choice*). It was tempting to quit at the point we knew it was a very good meeting. But we rarely did.

Each year we conducted a very intense planning cycle capped by a time we called Focus Week. During that week, we reviewed current-year performance across the key pillars of our performance, including our team, market, safety and quality, customer experience, and financial aspects. We also debated our strategies, the health of the organization, opportunities we were leaving unaddressed, and anything else that someone thought we needed to talk about to get better. In the fall of 2014, as we were going through the week, a person I had occasionally invited to observe these meetings pulled me aside. His job was to watch my leadership during this stressful week and give me feedback on leading with imagination. But before our feedback session, he wanted to understand the year we were having. He speculated that things must have been difficult given the critiques and drive for improvement he had observed.

"Actually," I said, "this is the best year we have ever had." This is what curiosity looks like combined with relentlessness and discipline. The first time you begin rationalizing how good you are, especially against competitors, you begin shortening the twenty-mile march. Next you start telling "Aren't we great" stories and sowing the seeds of future arrogance and failure. These are stories you should let your customers tell. This is when you should be asking even tougher questions. To do less than this is to play safe and hide. This is exactly the time to stay focused because the platform you have been building can finally be leveraged for more significant breakthroughs.

BURIED TREASURE

There is an unexpectedly high return on investment as you become curious about an organization's—and perhaps your own—mistakes. However, it is useful to recognize there are two types of mistakes. The first is commission, or taking a specific action that doesn't work. These are relatively easy to identify and well describe most of the discussion in the preceding section. The second type of mistake is omission, or *not* taking an action that was needed or would have produced a better outcome.

These mistakes of omission are difficult to spot and extremely difficult to measure to determine their magnitude. Accountants are very good at recording and sharing commissions from financial records, but they have few, if any, tools to calibrate the cost of omissions. The unfortunate truth of this fact set is that the errors of omission most often have much more severe and long-term consequences for an organization. For example, consider the story of Steve Sasson, who invented the digital camera while working for Kodak. He invented it twenty-five years before the digital camera drove Kodak to bankruptcy. Kodak chose *not* to embrace this technology at that time, nor later. Today this appears as an incredible error of omission, but that would ignore the context and environment of the time.

I recently had a conversation with the leader of an organization that specializes in helping companies that are part of industries going through transitions. She shared that even well-managed companies have high degrees of resistance to accepting the changes occurring around them. There is an overwhelming desire to protect the status quo, the current business model that has led to past success, and fear about the ability to lead in a new environment successfully. This is a powerful mix of story lines to keep us from taking risks to move to a new future.

This is where the treasure can be found if we stay intensely curious about our non-decisions. This is advanced work, so start small. I kept a list of decisions we (or I) didn't make and occasionally put an item on a meeting agenda. I would revisit one of the opportunities we'd passed on as a team and ask, "Did we make the right decision?" This was often uncomfortable, ripe with speculation and hidden assumptions, while seeming inefficient with our limited management time. Nonetheless, it was the groundwork for opening and expanding our capacity to imagine what might have been or could have happened. It also formed new patterns of cultural curiosity to protect against the status quo simply continuing as the status quo.

WHAT I KNOW ABOUT WOMEN

I am smiling at some of your expressions and the thought bubbles above your heads. You men are slightly intrigued, rather like the odd way we are drawn to a traffic slowdown and look at a car wreck on the side of the road. You women may be thinking, *Well, this should be a short section.*

I was at a conference half paying attention and half working on some project I needed to complete. Suddenly, something in the speaker's words caught my attention. The speaker was suggesting that we often do not understand the unique experiences that occur in our corporate suites. The truth is, it did not catch my attention because I found resonance. It was more like, *Huh? Could this be true? I think I know my team.*

However, I saw again a potential failure in my leadership— that dangerous place where I thought I was doing a good job valuing the team's diversity and leveraging it to the fullest (which sounds like what we just talked about, the same thing we do as organizations). After all, we had built one of the most diverse senior teams in our entire company. We had a number of strong women leaders, we had racial diversity, and we had seasoned and younger team members. We also had a diversity of experience and expertise. But the question kept nagging at me and would not relent.

Sometimes art and entertainment go above the superficial and offer a picture that points the way. I had recently watched the movie *The Butler*, a story based on the life of Eugene Allen (Cecil Gaines is the movie character), who became the head butler in the White House. Very early in the movie there is a difficult scene. Young Cecil Gaines is in the fields working alongside his father. The son of the plantation's owner takes Cecil's mother into a nearby shed and forces himself upon her while the work in the fields continues. Upon hearing the screams, Cecil looks at his father and, understanding little of the "nature of things" in the South at this time, implores his father to do something.

He confronts the owner's son as he walks past. It was only a question, not a threat or aggressive action. What happened next left me numb and cold. The man pulled a pistol and shot Cecil's father dead. (I later researched this particular event and discovered it was fictional and meant to portray a larger story.) It would be trite for me to say, "Wow. I understand how Cecil must feel." It would be nearly as trite to say I understand what it must have been like to be black at any time or at any place. The best I could hope to do is offer respect that others have a different walk than I do and occasionally find the courage to ask what another's experience might be while demonstrating an "authentic curiosity." And then earnestly listen without judgment or evaluation, but with empathy and openness.

I decided there was a group I had not thought about as intentionally as some: our female executives. We had begun preparing for a major launch of a women's program, including an investment in facilities of over $250 million to support the strategy. This was our next frontier of service, caring, and customer experience, with the benefit of gaining additional market share. The nagging question I couldn't shake at the conference was: how can we embark on this next journey as an organization if we don't even understand the experience of our female executive teammates?

I am sure I blundered my way through the next steps I took. I scheduled a late afternoon meeting outside the hospital so there wouldn't be a rush to the next meeting. The local coffee shop would work; it had a casual and relaxed atmosphere. Perfect— to encourage dialogue with the female executives. As you might imagine, given the unusual location and list of invitees, the executives began questioning my assistant regarding the purpose of the meeting. All she could offer was, "Brian wants to talk."

The day and time arrived. I was in trouble from the beginning. The coffee shop was full, so after awkwardly standing around and the women all looking at me like, "What is this about?" we decided to attach ourselves to the local diner. The diner staff looked at us with the same question: "What are you all doing here at three in the afternoon?" And "No, we don't want to eat, do you serve hot tea?" No. With that we ordered a round of iced teas and sodas. I waded in, awkwardly, and honestly curious.

They were understandably guarded for the first few minutes. But they quickly accepted the authenticity of the question, "What is it like as a female executive working at Florida Hospital?" They began to open up. Then my world was shaken up. I had limited insight into the differences they experienced. It ranged from being told earlier in their careers to dye their hair from blonde to brunette if you wanted to "make it" and be taken seriously to fearing being labeled if they were too direct or too emotional. Most poignant to me were the conversations they were rarely part of with the guys, and the two selves they had to be: one personality at work and another for home. Not to mention, they also experienced the burden, in most cases, for being the primary caregiver at home and executive at work. They described a world where they feel they must be better than the men on the same team to advance.

I didn't ask the question with a plan or next steps in mind. Curiosity is not always about an answer in the moment. It may be about noticing things and gradually seeing oneself—and those you work with or lead—more clearly and completely. I thought about how often we leave our full selves in pieces and fragmented in our work. I thought about how much of our human capacity, both personally and organizationally, is constrained by our assumptions and our biases. I left grateful that these gifted and successful women would share so honestly. I left regretful for all the missed opportunities to have led them better.

I drove home with one additional emotion and thought. It was humility for the sacrifices my wife has made for our family and for me by choosing to stay home and shoulder the burdens of raising five kids. She put her enormous talent and capability on the shelf for a time to serve us. I also understood the advantage I had in my career by her willingness to do this.

CURIOUS TO THE END

The team leading our largest campus faced a challenge. How do we engage our frontline staff to gain insight, find methods, and execute more consistently needed innovations and improvements? They built a learning lab that followed a concept called "design theory." One of the first tenets of design theory is the idea of empathy. The translation for me is being authentically curious about the customer or stakeholders of a process before determining the problem and especially the solution. It was an ongoing frustration how quickly we jumped right to a solution before we had fully gained an understanding of the problem. Even on the days we held ourselves up to better define the challenge, we almost never sought to be empathetically curious about our customers' experiences and perspectives. I was a fan of this lab and their thoughtful, love-based approach.

One of the most meaningful challenges they took on was the process women endured after a mammogram that did not yield a normal diagnosis. I have had the privilege to journey with several of my colleagues as their spouses were diagnosed with breast cancer. I have listened to their descriptions of getting that call: "We found something suspicious." Fewer things get said in a phone call that create more stress than these few words.

However, at least at that time in our care process, it routinely took twenty-eight days (and often over two months) to move from screening to diagnosis and a plan for treatment. This is a lifetime when you are facing a cancer diagnosis. The team set out with curiousity to learn more. They became curious on two fronts. First, they inquired about the perceptions of these women by conducting interviews, listening to their stories, and understanding the range of fears and concerns they had. On the second front, they explored quantitative empathy. They evaluated data, reviewed survey results, and mapped current state process end to end.

They added one additional innovative step: they brought in a partner (in this case, General Electric, or GE). General Electric makes a very impressive line of diagnostic X-ray equipment. Rarely does the company get close to the actual customer of the service. They were eager and engaged partners in this process and brought some of their best and brightest to learn alongside our team of clinicians and operators. This collaboration and process yielded a goal: take the process of screening, diagnosis, biopsy, pathology, and treatment from an average of twenty-eight days to just three! It took remaining curious, questioning every assumption, planned teamwork, change from every team member, and relentlessness, but, eventually, they reached their goal.

A GENERAL SOLUTION

One day as a team we decided it was time to pursue a global strategy. Healthcare is often said to be a local affair. This is true, in a sense. However, we believed there was an opportunity to compete for international business. Miami and Houston garner a large percentage of such business. The healthcare brand names such as Mayo, Cleveland Clinic, Massachusetts General Hospital, Johns Hopkins, and a few others get their share as well.

Florida Hospital was not a brand name, and Orlando was not a medical hub like Miami or Houston. However, we thought Orlando was a great destination and had something to offer. By this time, we had built a number of world-class programs. These were things people would travel for.

It was a Friday morning in a small conference room where we said it's time to stop talking about it and attack this opportunity. The next question from around the table was: What kind of person will it take to help get this done? We talked through the various skills we thought it would take. In a typical honest dialogue, we concluded it was not someone like us who operated hospitals. We needed someone different, but who? We jotted down a list: *understands the world, solves logistical problems, knows how to scale.*

The next Tuesday morning, I had breakfast with a friend who was serving as the ambassador to Luxembourg (a small but important country squeezed between Germany and Belgium). He started the conversation. "My friend is retiring in a few months, and do you think you might have something he could do for you?"

"Tell me more about your friend."

"He is a lieutenant general who is commander of the US Army in Europe."

I was intrigued, but it was not immediately apparent to me where a general, even one with three stars, without a medical background would fit into a healthcare organization. *Stay curious*, I thought to myself. I did know that under his command was Landstuhl Hospital, one of the Army's largest, a sacred place that is truly a miracle to behold, receiving most of the seriously wounded soldiers from the Iraq and Afghanistan battlefields.

Ambassador Robert Mandell looked straight at me and said, "Do you know what a general is good at?"

"What?" I asked.

"They are good at scale."

"I might have an idea," I quipped.

On a Sunday afternoon a few weeks later, I was standing on my back porch awaiting a call on my cell phone from the top US Army general in Europe, reporting to the NATO supreme commander. I still recall the strange feeling and the recurring thought: *How do you address a general?* I had never done that before.

The phone rang. I nervously answered. "Good afternoon, general."

"Please call me Mark."

Mark was Mark Hertling. Five months later, after his retirement ceremony and some well-deserved R and R, he showed up to my office with his Florida Hospital badge. He would often joke about being a soldier and now hanging out with healthcare people. Mark had a huge effect on all of us. It was largely a matter of curiosity that led a healthcare organization to explore the possibility of adding a military general to our senior team.

It wasn't always easy, but it was well worth the effort. Mark developed and launched our global strategy. He also took over our health- and fitness-related businesses. It made sense, as he had been recently appointed by President Barack Obama to serve on his Council for Fitness. But, probably, the most important work Mark did was with our physicians. Dr. Dave Moorhead and I felt strongly that we had to get more physicians into leadership roles if we wanted to continue our journey on quality and safety and to make the transitions we thought were going to be essential for the next expectations of healthcare providers.

But doctors are rarely trained for these roles. Mark had a phrase he often used: "If you want a seat at the table, then you need to learn table manners." This formed the basis for his approach. And it suited Dr. Moorhead and me just fine. Most of the programs we had previously reviewed were of the mini-MBA version: good technical skills about organizational and business processes, but we needed leaders. Little existed at the time, so Mark and the team went to work and created an innovative program and method of developing physician leaders. I highly recommend his book, *Growing Physician Leaders*, which tells more of that story.

I have often joked with him that he should publish another with a different title, a book on leadership, period. In fact, on a road trip my wife took with my two youngest daughters, who were sixteen and fourteen at the time, they read Mark's book out loud. They loved it. It will challenge anyone who reads it and will further encourage your leadership curiosity.

A SPOONFUL OF STRUCTURE

I would like to share a few closing thoughts about curiosity. First, be authentic. Practice presence and being truly interested in the answers to the questions you ask. My own wiring is often to ask the question but then be thinking about or eager to debate the answer rather than listening. It is something to be careful about. It often takes people a while to believe you really want to know what they think. Be patient and persistent, with yourself and with others.

We started a leadership advisory team in which we invited about fifteen directors to meet monthly with me. Sometimes it was an open-ended question about how things are going. How are we doing communicating? What might we do differently? Other times, we had a decision we needed to make, and we would give them our assumptions and fact sets, explain our logic and considerations, and ask what they thought. Earlier I'd mentioned the debrief we did after our leader conferences with our senior team, but we also did it with this team. They were the intended audience, after all.

I realized how important really listening was when we first assembled this group and as we were approaching our next leadership conference. We shared the proposed agenda with them, the messages we thought needed to be delivered, and how we intended to accomplish it all. They gave us plenty of feedback. In the end, we incorporated the majority of it. When we met after the meeting and asked for their feedback, they shocked me. First, they said they were surprised I had asked for their input. More telling, they were completely shocked that we had listened and incorporated their input into the day. It struck me how much corporate conditioning must have already existed for us to be surprised at this feedback.

I'd also experienced similar conditioning when senior leaders asked for feedback. What they really meant was: *We would like your concurrence and compliance. We are happy to make minor tweaks and improvements. But, again, mostly what we are asking for is your enthusiastic support for our plan.*

I am guessing that most of you can recount times when you experienced this, or, if you are like me, the times you did this to others. Please don't be harsh as you remember those moments. There is a reason why there is such a lack of curiosity in leaders. It is hard. In his book *Curious: The Desire to Know and Why Your Future Depends on It*, Ian Leslie speaks to the heart of why: "Curiosity is unruly. It doesn't like rules, or, at least, it assumes that all rules are provisional, subject to the laceration of a smart question nobody has yet thought to ask. It disdains the approved pathways, preferring diversions, unplanned excursions, impulsive left turns. In short, curiosity is deviant." Managers have an instinct to control, and curiosity is hard to control. Leaders learn to manage their impulses to control the deviance of curiosity for the return it offers.

The last thing I suggest to strengthen your leadership in the area of curiosity is to use structure to your advantage. There is no shortage of great questions and very little need, at least at the beginning, to invent your own. During our efforts to qualify for the Malcolm Baldrige National Quality Award site visit, we learned a series of questions that served as guides to understanding and improving our efforts around innovation, which, frankly, required an organizational curiosity.

Another great tool we used was the Doblin Model of Innovation. There are others, but I came to appreciate this one. It identifies ten types of innovation. Its application will be different in every industry and company. The insight for healthcare was that the vast majority of innovation in our industry was in technology. Collectively, we virtually ignored the other nine types. I believe there are two major consequences to this. The first is a poor return on innovation and investment. Technology innovation in healthcare produces the least return. It is expensive, easy for others to purchase and duplicate, and rarely lives up to the hype. The second is the lack of fundamental innovation in the industry around the increasing cost of care.

As healthcare providers, we are too eager to purchase equipment and computer software while we miss opportunities to explore innovation in the value of our product performance, experience, service, distribution channels, business model structures, and so forth. We keep playing the same game and wondering why we are not driving costs down or adding new and useful value like other industries. We learned at Florida Hospital that if you are relentlessly curious to the point of insight, then it becomes possible to create multiple types of innovations. It does not lessen the challenge to execute, but it does increase the odds of sustained market success.

It is worth repeating Ken Robinson's insight, delivered in one of the most-watched TED Talks, "The role of a creative leader is not to have all the ideas; it's to create a culture where everyone can have ideas and feel that they are valued." And that happens in two ways in order to lead with imagination. First, you must understand that useful and original ideas are not random. They come most often out of a process. It is your job to understand and facilitate that process. The second way is by creating the environment for curiosity. This gives people the chance to do and be their best.

If you are leading from love, how could you want less for your people?

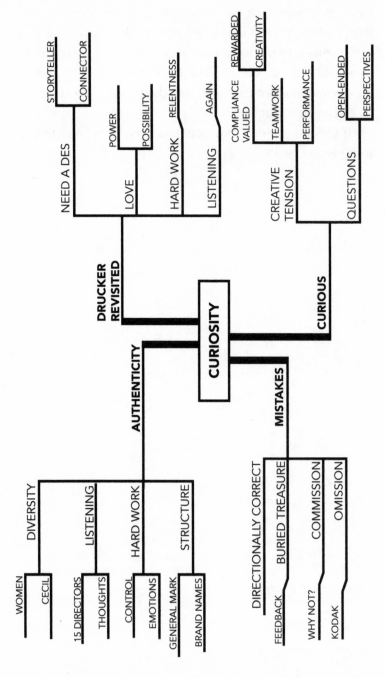

FROM HA HA…TO AHA

THE MISUNDERSTANDING
ABOUT HUMOR

"A sense of humor is part of the art of leadership, of getting along with people, of getting things done." —*Dwight D. Eisenhower*

LEADERSHIP LYRIC

CREATIVE CONCEPT: THE PUNCH LINE

Humor is evoked when a trigger, contained in the punch line, causes an audience to abruptly shift its understanding of the story from an obvious story line to an unexpected interpretation. It opens the mind and heart to new thinking, while delighting with surprise.

SUMMARY

Laughter creates a runway for love to land on, and then take off again. Life is serious, to be sure. Organizations are serious, too, but they are made up of humans. And because of that, humor contributes an essential living element to culture. Humor makes us human. It connects us. It gives us energy and capacity to handle stress and challenge. It lifts us. If we believe people are our greatest organizational capacity, then infusing humor into an enterpise is a high return on investment and undervalued as a creative and cultural force. Humor opens a pathway to breakthroughs and new insights. It becomes a competitive advantage.

AS WITH MOST THINGS

My wife is the funniest person I know. She is constantly looking for the funny. I can't tell you how many times I have watched her tell a story that had the room erupting in laughter with the result that everyone in the room resonated with the universal truth of her tale, feeling connected and fully human. Her humor has had a positive impact on our children. I have seen tears turn to laughter as she listens, very empathetically, and then says something that brings the giggles bubbling out from deep inside. I have seen her use a comical observation to turn a tense and potentially disruptive situation into a manageable one.

I, on the other hand, have never thought of myself as funny. After all, I am a finance guy and an executive, with a seriousness from the day I was born. However, it turns out I am able to observe and understand that humor has power. Humor gives us the ability to change the dynamics of a situation. It also helps us relate to and connect with people. Even a guy like me can learn, with a little help and practice, to set the right tone in the workplace, where people are relaxed and engaged.

I am not talking about becoming a stand-up comedy genius like Jerry Seinfeld or Jim Gaffigan, or an improv guru like Drew Carey. I have learned that even if you are not funny, you can learn to be observant and look for humor. This is what improv classes teach. It is a learned skill, like most things.

Here is an example. I was driving to one of our "all-campus" leadership meetings. During the drive, I noticed a series of billboards for the Universal Studios amusement park. On the last one was a picture of the Incredible Hulk roller coaster emblazoned with something like "A scream a minute." So when I opened the meeting, I shared how we had been talking about best idea wins and how collaboration increases our probabilities for success in the marketplace. I remained very serious in my tone.

Then I transitioned to the billboard I had observed driving to the meeting. I reminded them of our next strategic push to elevate our women's services with new facilities and an improved patient experience to match the physical structures. Then I shared that I had worked out our ad campaign for the launch after seeing the Incredible Hulk billboard. We would revolutionize our obstetrics program with a billboard that read, "Florida Hospital, delivering your baby...with a scream a minute." Slow laughter began building as they realized I had sucked them in, and then it erupted when someone from the marketing team yelled out, "Keep your day job!"

We were off to a great meeting. Everyone was relaxed and at ease. More importantly, everyone was engaged and ready to contribute fully to the meeting.

Over time, while I served as the chief financial officer, it became my habit to begin financial reports and discussions at these same meetings with a story. Knowing my limitations, I relied on my wife's talent as a comedy writer and her co-creation on the flow and phrasing of these stories. Usually it was a story that highlighted some personal shortcoming. The result was always positive; it had a humanizing effect. I began to grasp how effective humor was in setting the stage for creativity, connection, and insight in a business setting.

When I became the operational leader, I struggled with whether highlighting my personal shortcomings made sense in this new, higher-profile role. I knew that, as the former CFO, many people thought it had been a mistake to place me in that role. I worried that telling stories about myself could become fuel for that view. After all, it was my job to drive strategy and facilitate the creation of the roadmap to our future and then execute it. How could the guy who tells stories about making a mess of a family vacation be trusted to lead the planning and strategy process?

At my first "all-campus" meeting as COO, I shared the following story with the disclaimer, "Don't try this at home."

My anniversary was approaching, and, as I was looking at the calendar, I realized it was on Tuesday. Tuesday seemed an odd day to celebrate our anniversary, so I mentioned it to my wife. She was quick to grasp my unspoken processing, and, given her own busy week, suggested we not celebrate on Tuesday but hold for the weekend.

I shared with the team that I thought this was a workable solution. I further went on to explain that, in my one-track processing, I had also concluded that when you agree to celebrate your Tuesday anniversary on Saturday, that is exactly what it means. Yes, I can already feel some of you shaking your heads, and I think I see your judgmental expressions. I know that because that is what I saw looking into the audience at this point in the story. I should have just quit and let them create their own ending.

I continued though.

"It turns out that when you agree to celebrate a special occasion on a different day than the day it actually is, what that means is you are really going to celebrate it twice but with different levels of intensity."

It was a hit. Almost every man in the room had made a similar mistake and expressed solidarity that we were not alone. They were not the only unthinking male on the planet. Strangely to me, the women also appreciative, almost admiringly pleased that I would acknowledge this failing of the male perspective.

The real message that my audience got wasn't that I was funny. (I did mention I had a good writer.) The message was that I was a real person, and that I could, in fact, be trusted. It added credibility to this early phase of operational leadership.

REINFORCING, REFLECTING, AND RETELLING

Our human souls want to laugh, and it doesn't take much to get people started. Once people start laughing, it's contagious. Laughter is also connective and a very effective lubricant against organizational friction, stress, and circumstance. A recent *Forbes* article summarized some of the research on laughter:

Laughter is a potent endorphin releaser.
Laughter contagiously forms social bonds.
Laughter fosters brain connectivity.
Laughter is central to relationships.
Laughter has an effect similar to antidepressants.
Laughter protects your heart.

Who wouldn't want more of each of these benefits of laughter? But this is more than a nicety. My experience is that when significant stress comes to us (as individuals or as organizations), this medicine plays a crucial part in giving a *benefit of the doubt*. This benefit of the doubt keeps us focused on solving problems and creating solutions instead of attacking one another and placing blame.

I believe that these shared moments of laughter create a contagion that is organic and produces a powerful dynamic. When leaders work (yes, it is work) to foster laughter, it is a step toward the "aha" moments of inspiration. It has been said it is a short step from ha ha to aha.

In addition to the stories I told at our leadership meetings, our chief people officer, Ed Hodge, decided to push us further down the funny track. His idea was succinct and straightforward. In an effort to divide the daylong meeting and give people a break between the intense discussions on topics such as budgets, strategy, competitive environment, and operational performance, he produced a series of videos *loosely based* on the agenda's topics to run during the transitions.

My favorite video involved our chief financial officer Eddie Soler and several of his senior finance officers, at least the male ones. It was a sequence of the CFO advising his team about one of the secrets to his success (mentoring). That secret was regular visits to the salon to have his nails done. The filming was superb, with all the finance guys at a local spa reading magazines while their feet soaked and their finger nails were being filed. The final shot was the CFO handing the monthly financial report to the division CEO, who remarked about how nice his nails looked and asked where he'd had them done. The film shot of his hand sliding the report across the desk, taking up the entire screen, brought the house down.

It makes total sense. If you are a CFO handing financial reports to other senior leaders, make sure your hands are in great shape. Wait, what? Everything was wrong about this. But the finance team became real, poking fun at themselves, and during the budget season, that opened an easier dialogue. We had real work and hard work to get done, but some fun along the way didn't make us less serious about completing the task. In fact, we were focused on the task and not on one another, as is so often the case in a budget process. And oh, how many times people retold and laughed again as they replayed the scenes in their minds. We even held a final session with the team to watch all the videos again.

We built on each humor experiment, kept learning, and kept trying things. Every December, we planned a holiday banquet for our medical staff. It was a popular affair regularly attracting almost a thousand people. The format was dinner, a few remarks by the president of the medical staff and myself, followed by entertainment. Our budget did not allow us to hire the most current entertainment options, but, still, they were always successful, polished artists. However, once the program started, about a third of the doctors would get up and leave.

Driving home after one of these events, I shared with my wife how this annoyed me. I knew these physicians had early schedules the next morning, but still. We talked about the challenge of finding the right genre of music to make everyone happy and willing to stay. As she has so often done, she broke through to an idea: "Why don't you try hiring a comedian?"

We did exactly that the following year—Sinbad, as I recall—it was quite the event. *No one left.* Sinbad was so good we even hired him again a few years later. I was glad people stayed, but there was more to appreciate. The next day, the doctors repeated half the show to one another, laughing again, building connections to the organization and one another. And, even better, they didn't have to work at it, and it didn't require a program or training event away from taking care of patients. I imagine they were even sharing some of the jokes with their patients. Laughter became medicine, perhaps.

I am intrigued with the last benefit of humor listed in the *Forbes* article: "Laughter protects your heart." I shared some of my story about dealing with heart disease in chapter 4, and so this caught my attention. However, I wonder if the most potent possibility out of laughter is connected to chapter 3 and the role our hearts play in love. This is the point of these stories, and I am convinced that laughter is fertile soil for love to grow, personally and organizationally.

FIRE IN THE HOLE

The work to foster humor at the organizational level is critical, but eventually, it has to show up in the day-to-day working environment and team dynamics. This is where the culture becomes rich and the power to perform accelerates. I would listen for the evidence that this was happening. On many days, you could hear the laughter and lightheartedness around the organization. I listened for it both in successful and stressful times. It is an essential ingredient in each case.

Sometimes I was even blessed to experience the humor first-hand. It started with a busy morning out of the office. I had an amazing assistant in Becky Villanueva, who, in addition to being efficient and organized, made me laugh regularly. Sometimes this started with her giving me a forceful command that made me wonder who really worked for whom. As I passed her desk and headed to my office on that particular day, she suspected I was in my habit of wandering around and forgetting to tell her. So she said, "Don't disappear. Sheryl needs to see you urgently. I will call her to come up."

Sheryl Dodds was the chief clinical officer and one of the most genuine and caring people you will ever meet. I thought of her as Saint Sheryl. Naturally, I was anxious about what had happened while I was away. It is often the nature of the hospital world that when either your senior physician or clinical officer needs to see you ASAP, it usually isn't good. When Sheryl arrived, the laughter was spilling out and she could barely contain herself. She had brought Ms. Lee Johnson, Dr. Moorhead's extremely able operating executive, with her. She was amused as well, though slightly more controlled.

Well, at least we didn't have a crisis. But what we did have was still a mystery because neither of them could stop laughing long enough to catch their breath to speak. Impatiently, and now laughing myself at nothing except their laughter, I said, "Whaaaaaaat?"

They began to unpack "the event." Dr. Dave Moorhead, the chief medical officer of one of the largest hospital operations in the country, and Lieutenant General Mark Hertling, former US Army commander for Europe and senior vice president at

Florida Hospital, had come up with the enlightened idea of lighting fireworks in Dave's office.

Some context is important: I was traveling through Tennessee, the home of some unbelievable fireworks that are seemingly illegal in most of the other forty-nine states. So I stopped at a fireworks store. Something you have to know about Mark: he avoids impressive descriptions of himself, introducing himself as a soldier and then a tanker. Yes, the first part of his career he served in a tank division. As I was picking out our New Year's Eve fireworks, I saw a package of small fireworks shaped like tanks. I had no idea what kind of pyrotechnics they produced but decided to buy a couple and present them to Mark as a gift, which I did when I returned to work after the holidays.

To this day, I do not know whose idea it was to fire up one of the tanks in Dave's office. These two very gifted men assumed that once the tank's fuse was lit, it would simply roll across the long conference table and fizzle out. I also don't know where they got matches or a lighter, but once they had the fuse lit, the small tank began to spin wildly. Unable to gain control and grab it, it careened off the table and onto Dave's expensive Persian rug he had brought back from his time serving as a hospital CEO in Saudi Arabia.

"Well, that can't be good," I stated, trying to maintain an executive composure.

Sheryl continued. Next thing, smoke began pouring into the air. People from nearby offices came into Dave's office, prepared to pull the fire alarm before it went off on its own. Lee and Sheryl came to the rescue, assessing no fire was actually present they began waving magazines and notepads to disperse the smoke. Once the possibility of the fire alarm going off and the subsequent investigation by the fire department into the events of this tank brigade were averted, the ladies could barely wait to tell me. For days, they were still breaking into laughter every time they passed Dave or Mark's office.

Dave and Mark's laughter came a little later. They had crafted a story that had placed me at the center of blame for providing faulty tanks. Now, don't get me wrong. I am not advocating playing with fireworks at the office. Nor would Mark and Dave. (I believe they learned their lesson as later that day, I saw them in the parking lot lighting the remaining tank.) What I am suggesting is that play and laughter authentically born have an important place in the pursuit of imagination. Learning not to take ourselves and our roles too seriously (the work, yes) is a strong predictor of future creativity and innovation. And it creates connection for those events that require all hands on deck.

ACT II

A test of our culture and progress was closing in on us. In chapter 6, I talked about failing our Joint Commission Survey and then moving our accreditation to the DNV. I mentioned that we passed our next survey with flying colors, but there was a rest of the story to tell. We were all on a heightened alert and in a ready state for our next survey. Although it had been almost three years since our last survey, the memories were fresh for me and the rest of the teams preparing for a surprise visit. We had been given an approximate window when they would arrive, so each Monday for weeks, we had a phone chain set up to alert the organization if they arrived.

At 7:30 a.m. on this particular Monday, my phone went off on the drive into the hospital.

"Let me guess, 'they' are here," I said.

"Yes, they are. We need you at the opening conference to greet them at 8:15."

"I will be there," I answered, with an increased energy more than typical first thing on a Monday morning. I saw this as a test to measure our progress over the last several years. It is one thing to think you are getting better or making progress. However, it is quite another to have to prove it to an objective and independent group of surveyors. Truth, even if painful, is better than illusion or worse, delusion. And I believed we were ready.

The opening conference was nothing other than ordinary as these meetings go. A little "put your best foot forward" and a dose of "Florida Hospital hospitality" and we were done at 9 a.m. sharp. Surveyors are not overly fond of chitchat, preferring to be on the floors tracing the patients' care through all our processes. Besides, we were all in for a very long week. At 9:20 a.m., my phone rang again. Perhaps a quick debrief from the session just finished. No. Chief medical and chief clinical officers needed to see me immediately, and they were bringing the chief information officer as well. That is a lot of chiefs in the room, and it didn't seem good.

In less than five minutes, they were all standing in my office. Our computer system just crashed. I thought a moment, contemplating how to respond. I don't always *contemplate* my responses, but I was keenly aware of my failure during the last time the surveyors were here. I had the sense to know that, and as the leader, my response would set a tone. In my head, I walked the logic chain through: there are 365 days a year, and there are three years between surveys. Therefore, there had been 1,095 days for our computers to go down (which they never had) since our last survey, and yet today they did. You can't make this stuff up.

I burst into laughter.

Their faces suggested that was not the response they were expecting.

"This is awesome." I said. "Do you guys realize how much more we will learn about how far we have come, or not? I can't believe our luck," or something close to that, was my response.

So why does humor matter? Because our computers were down for almost two days of the survey. Well over half our nurses had never taken care of a patient without one. They had never seen a paper chart. We were solving basic problems like how to get lab results to the emergency department while another team was working with the company that housed and operated our clinical computer system to get us back online.

I believe the surveyors were impressed by our clinical care under these difficult conditions, but even more so by the teams' attitudes. Not one time did I hear or see finger pointing. Laughter was still echoing in the hallways, perhaps even more so. There was a de-stressing of a very stressful situation, built on the bonds previously developed and strengthened in the crucible of this momentary crisis.

We passed and by the surveyors' own words at the closing, with flying colors. I think they even said they were proud of us. Not the typical language of surveyors.

There were two clear payoffs from this experience. We confirmed we were making progress in our culture, and it was benefitting patients. There was a clear and palpable resiliency evident in the capacity of the organization. This picture of the power of humor and laughter contributes to a clear competitive advantage—one more hard turn on the flywheel of who we were becoming.

Oh, and the second bonus. It turns out we had negotiated a clause with the computer company that if the computers ever went down for more than an hour, we were due a refund for every hour after that. We were down for almost forty-eight hours. I was part of negotiating that clause, and we all believed it was a "nothing" clause because the likelihood of it ever happening was insignificant.

When the check arrived for over $300,000, we laughed all the way to the bank. We'd gotten paid to test ourselves.

THE LAST LAUGH

It is far too easy, of course, to misunderstand and undervalue humor. It is so universal, it's similar to water. Water gives life, yet we so often take it for granted until we have a shortage. I remember a backpacking trip where this happened to my long-time friend and me. We became obsessed with conserving our water. We wouldn't cook our meals because they required water, so we could save it to drink. We cut our trip short in our thirst to find water. When we did find it, it was gold. Laughter is the same. It is everywhere and seemingly limitless—until it's not. When it all but disappears from the hallways, it leaves an eerie silence. I have said it before but leading with imagination is about fully embracing the power of people. It is about unleashing their fullest potential. In order to do that, you need laughter as an ally.

Margaret Wheatley tells that, "Nobel Prize winner Sir Peter Medawar said that scientists build "explanatory structures, telling stories which are scrupulously tested to see if they are stories about real life." I like this idea of storytellers. It works well to describe all of us. We are great weavers of tales, listening intently around the campfire to see which stories best capture our imagination and the experience of our lives. If we can look at ourselves truthfully in the light of this fire and stop being so serious about getting things "right—as if there were still an objective reality out there—we can engage in life differently, more playfully."

We bring both our wounds and our wonder from child-hood and life to work. Being willing and eager to laugh gives wonder more space and keeps our wounds in their place. They say laughter is the best medicine but it's also an expression of love. Maybe, by this expression, we give up control, realizing we cannot stop the rain, all the while realizing we sure as hell can learn to laugh and dance in it.

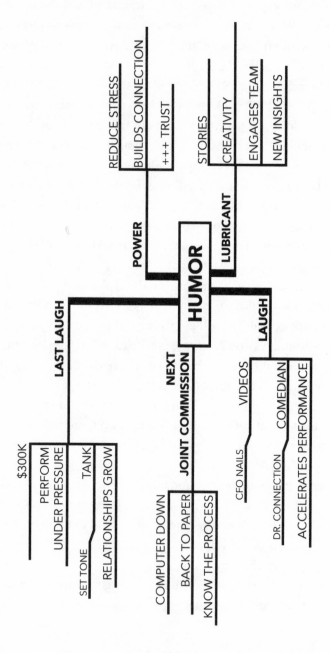

Connecting the Dots

DOING WHATEVER IT TAKES

> "It's not what you look at that matters,
> it's what you see." —*Henry David Thoreau*

LEADERSHIP LYRIC

CREATIVE CONCEPT: THE LONG LINE

The long line is the force that propels a musical piece forward
and keeps it energized and alive. Think of it like grabbing
your shirt and pulling you through to the end. It applies
to books, movies ("I don't want to go to the restroom and
miss anything"), storytelling, and even social media.

SUMMARY

Leadership is hard work. Leading with imagination and
leading for results require skill and competence, constant
self-evaluation, a servant's heart, and a relentlessness to get
it "mostly" right. It is about asking the important and difficult
questions of yourself and of the organization and waiting for
the answers. It is about engaging and encouraging what is
working and owning and dealing with what is not. It is about
finding the way and doing whatever job needs to be done
to support the team. It is about continuously and consistently imagining the vision, communicating it, and taking
daily action toward it. Benjamin Zander, conductor of the

Boston Philharmonic Orchestra, has described the "long line" or vision of a musical piece. He explains how the "line" is easily lost with too much attention to single notes or short passages. As leaders, it is our constant job to keep bringing our organizations and enterprises back to the long line of the music and connecting the dots back to the big why.

CAKE

There is a worn-out phrase which goes something like this: "_____ is the icing on the cake." I think this is wrong. I love carrot cake. I cannot imagine it without that cream-cheese icing and the little frosting carrot embedded on top. Icing, for most of us, is not simply nice to have but is a necessary part of the cake. It brings the whole thing called *cake* to its best presentation and experience.

It is the same with connecting the dots as the leader. It may seem like a nice thing, a finishing touch, after the strategy is decided, the goals are set, and the budget completed. We have walked through the journey of leading with imagination from love to laughter. However, if you fail to engage in connecting the dots for your people, your leadership cake will be incomplete. This is where the *art* of leadership is most required and becomes most evident.

This phase of the journey begins with our friend from chapter 4, Robert Greenleaf, and his concept of servant leadership. The first word is *servant*, not *leader*. Connecting the dots is about serving your team, your customers, and your communities before serving the organization or yourself.

THE BIG WHY

Noted author, speaker, and marketing consultant Simon Sinek, in his bestselling book *Start with Why*, speaks to this fundamental point. If you want people to show up to work fully engaged and inspired, you have to start with why. How, what, when, and where are not enough for most people. Our human nature is looking for something to believe in, to be part of, that is bigger than us, and that matters.

Simon explains that customers buy "why" you do something, and so do your people. It is the bigger purpose, and it's what connects and sustains the way forward for most of us.

GETTING TO THE CORE, GETTING CLEAR

The idea of The Big Why will lead us to what is core to the organization. Another way to put it might be in the question: What is our mission? The real one, as we discussed earlier. Once we have the core in front of us, we must be clear about what it looks like, how it shows up in big and little things, and what actions support it. I am sure, if you think a bit, you have been in an organization where how people behaved, especially leaders, was very different from the espoused mission statements.

It is essential to articulate The Big Why and core values of the organization and then stay relentless in keeping them front and center with discipline and consistency. Let's look back for a moment to explore this connect-the-dots idea. Remember the story in chapter 5 about transforming the emergency department? We had decided this was a mission-critical project to change the thinking across the whole of the enterprise. We were making only minor progress when we came to a conclusion after asking some of those important questions and working hard to really listen. The conclusion was that fixing the EDs wasn't a clear goal.

The "why" was mostly in my head. The goal was vague. The specific and organizing efforts were not clear. So back to the drawing board. You also may recall the question that started with "What does the patient want when they come to the ED?" Answer: to see a doctor. That became our goal. Why? Because that is what our patients most wanted and needed. And even more compelling, because lives would be saved. Our patients might be relieved of pain, their worries and fears calmed, and their treatment started sooner. It was what we all would have wanted if it were us or our loved ones in this circumstance.

With the "why" articulated and accepted by the team, we were able to get to more productive work. But now our actions had to support this approach. It started with a discipline *not* to ask all the same questions we used to ask, e.g., labor standards and budget explanations, customer satisfaction questions, and many more. We only asked one question: What was the door-to-doctor time? We resisted asking those other questions for over a year.

You see, we had to trust our people now that they had The Big Why. We had to trust that they cared about their patients as much as we administrators did. This isn't that hard if you take the time to know the team. And we had to trust the process. Not doing this would have been like planting a garden and then pulling up a plant by its roots every day to check its progress.

I would like to tell you that at this point that everything fell into place. It didn't. There is a harsh reality to this leading thing, and particularly leading with imagination. Everything is hard. Things don't naturally line up to move things to an objective. The universe mostly doesn't seem to care about your goals.

While we learned to trust our people and processes, we realized our people were incredible. What wasn't incredible were our processes. We as leaders had not been disciplined to assure they were fully effective to achieve the desired outcome. It was our job to support our teams and caregivers with processes that supported them. One more cycle of improvement.

PROCESS, PROCESS, PROCESS

One of the most significant challenges of leading with imagination is clarifying your thinking to understand that processes support people, not the other way around. It is back to that compliance thing: better not to rock the boat challenging the process than to push back on something that isn't working.

As leaders, we are often quick to give orders, place demands, and create expectations with little understanding of the processes that will support the people we placed these requirements on. We neglect the hard work of assuring they have the tools, resources, and mechanisms to achieve the goals. And we forget far too often to go back to The Big Why both for the clarity and inspiration needed.

If we are to connect the dots, we must consistently keep going back to the process. It is one of the core competencies of our friends down the road at Disney and is exemplified by the example of the team member selling ice cream. Disney designed the process so that a team member charged with selling ice cream has everything he or she needs to be great at selling ice cream. The process is designed to provide an ice cream cart stocked with product, available power nearby to keep the cart cold, the tender systems to conveniently transact the money exchange, and a leader who routinely engages with the team member to assure they have all available resources to succeed at the goal. In healthcare, at least, we often get this wrong and leave doctors and nurses to manage too many subprocesses, resulting in ineffective connection with patients.

THOSE DAMN SILOS

Silos are great if you live in the Midwest on a farm. They serve a very useful purpose by storing grain. But they are also very dangerous. Over time, the grain in a silo produces methane gas. If farmers enter the silo without taking precautions, they can be silently suffocated.

Silos are a constant problem in organizations. Perhaps this is a good analogy to consider. Silos have a purpose to organize and store resources, but if not managed with a great deal of precaution, they will also suffocate teamwork, creativity, innovation, and performance.

In our journey concerning the processes required to support the emergency department results we all desired, it became clear that two supporting departments, or "silos," were critical: the laboratory and radiology. Both provided very valuable information in determining a diagnosis. However, the problem was the speed at which the information for treatment became available. At first we didn't even know how fast or slow it was.

The laboratory was quick to put a system in place to begin measuring the turnaround of lab results. Once that was in place, in partnership with the ED nurses and doctors, they began to define and refine the process to improve the results and speed things up.

On the other hand, radiology took a more siloed approach. They indeed put a process in place to begin measuring. But when we began exploring their turnaround times as a team, something wasn't adding up. They had reported, independently of the ED, that their turnaround times were very good and that, if there was a problem, it must be in the ED—not radiology.

As senior leaders began to break down the silos as part of connecting the dots, we began to see the disconnect. Because the lab had partnered with the ED with a clear sense of the "bigger why," they chose to measure turnaround time from the point at which lab work was drawn in the ED, and then at each stage of the process, e.g., how long from initial draw until sent to the lab, how long from arrival in lab until test performed. This measuring continued until results were delivered and read by the physician.

In radiology, they only measured their performance from the time the test was read by the radiologist (physician) until those results were delivered back to the ED. While this is an important sub-measure, it ignored the two most significant bottlenecks in the process: getting the test performed and then getting those images in front of the radiologist to read.

I don't think they were trying to hide or not support; they were just thinking in a silo. This illustrates one of the important jobs of a leader: keeping silos at bay—keeping the team focused on The Big Why and the end game so no one suffocates.

STANDING IN THE GAPS

I don't think a day exists when you get it *all* right. On our best days, and only for a fleeting moment, we might approximate getting everything right. So that truth creates another essential task in connecting the dots. When values are unfulfilled, or the process fails to do its job, we as leaders must stand in the gap. We must work to name the gap and then muster the courage to do something about it.

With our corporate bureaucracies trying to maintain control and compliance, we are often put in a tough spot to challenge it for the sake of our people, the organization's performance, and, ultimately, the customers we serve. This truth has a way of hiding from us rather frequently. Too many times, I have heard leaders tell those they lead, "Just do it. That is what management wants." Gone is The Big Why, gone are the espoused values, gone are the customers' needs, and gone is caring for our people.

Several years into fixing the ED's journey, after we had made consistent and steady progress with clear processes operating and a vibrant culture throughout, we ran into one of these gaps. It is a very sensitive topic and one full of potholes and unintended consequences: bonuses.

The prior year, we had decided it would make sense to set up a formalized staff bonus criteria. We had an informal one of sorts, but we had gotten plenty of feedback that it always seemed a mystery how they were determined. Staff were always appreciative but were nonetheless confused about what we were rewarding or reinforcing. So the human resource team went to work. They solicited feedback from staff and leaders alike.

Bonus plans always have a risk related to messaging, so almost as important as deciding what to do is trying to anticipate these other consequences. We created a simple two-part formula. One half was based on customer feedback for inpatient care and the other half for emergency-department-experience scores. We were rather pleased, as I remember, for the plan's simplicity, the clarity around a "big why," and the belief that this measure was directly within the staff's control.

But then an unexpected thing happened. Our volumes grew well beyond what we anticipated. Our emergency department's word-of-mouth reputation was growing. We began taking market share—lots of it. We grew almost 10 percent, an enormous amount for any hospital. We were not staffed for such growth, it was straining all of our operating processes, and it just kept coming.

We finished the year well ahead on our financial budget. But as we coped with the day-to-day challenges of a staffing shortage, capacity and space limits, and strained processes, we missed our ED patient experience targets. Not by much, but still we missed them. We had moved the culture from excuse-making it had once done very effectively to one that rarely used them. Our way of honest assessment was found in the famous line spoken by Yoda to young Luke Skywalker: "Do or do not. There is no try."

The second challenge was in the way the organization determined the bonuses for different levels of the hierarchy. Executive bonuses were determined at the parent corporation. It skewed toward a bonus based on financial metrics. The director and manager plans, on the other hand, were determined at the hospital-system level and were equally balanced between financial and customer metrics. And as I previously described, the staff bonuses were based solely on customer metrics.

You likely already see the bad setup. Executives earned almost all of their bonus potential as a result of the strong financial outcomes due to the volume growth and efficient use of resources. Directors and managers fared okay, but not as well as executives. And the staff, well—sorry, those are the rules.

We struggled with the idea of changing the rules and communicating a message that performance doesn't *really* matter. It was a reasoned concern in a disciplined and performance-driven organization. We struggled over credibility with our corporate sponsors. Much of the rest of the corporation did not even have a staff bonus plan, and here we were considering paying out even when we didn't meet the targets.

In the end we concluded that our methodology was inadequate to recognize the enormous load the staff had carried. It didn't acknowledge that they had never quit on the goal. They just kept working as a team to find a way through to best care for *their* patients, so we resolved to pay the bonus. We also resolved to do more than the calculations called for so the message would not be lost on The Big Why. It was our way as an executive team to say more than, "You met the goal," but, "Thank you for not relenting."

Of course, we acknowledged the flaw of the bonus structure in an extraordinary year. And we enjoyed the process of celebrating in a series of events all over the organization that were filled with creative ways of saying thank you. I truly believe the executives and leadership team enjoyed saying thank you at least as much as the staff appreciated hearing and experiencing it.

METHODS EVEN IN MADNESS

There are those moments when all the inputs produce an output that, in quiet confidence, says *wow*. The was the day Vip said yes. Vip is Dr. Vipul Patel, one of the world's leading urologists, performing robotically assisted prostatectomies. In simpler words, he removes cancerous prostates with incredible results in what is called the trifecta, maintaining sexual function, continence, and eliminating the cancer.

One of our executives had found Dr. Patel as a result of her family's healthcare journey. She came back after this experience with a radical idea, that this no-name hospital, outside of a strong academic core, should recruit the world's leading robotic-assisted surgeon in urology. I must admit it seemed a stretch, but two things drove our thinking to attempt it. First, we had been developing our team-building capacity, and we had been experimenting with an innovation model that suggested innovation was most productive when several types of innovation were combined. This recruitment and the plan to build a prostate center would provide an opportunity to test both our team-building capacity and innovation model.

Unlike any recruitment we had ever done, this one was a team effort. Usually one or two executives were involved with financial oversight of the final deal. To attract a talent like Vip, this would take a full-court press by a diverse team. It required the executive with the initial relationship, and the leader for the Celebration campus (in fact, it would change almost everything on this campus). The planning and marketing group were heavy players to build the brand and market this new prostate center.

Not far behind were the fundraising team, the physician-training center (as Vip would be a leader in the center, teaching other surgeons his technique), and, critically, the physician group and hospital operations, as well as the finance team. We had never done such a comprehensive recruitment requiring a major investment in both the physician and his teams' cost, but also future building and equipment expenditures. The effort raised eyebrows throughout the company and at the corporate offices. Many saw the possibility of reputation failure and financial disaster—a big risk. I was okay with these opinions because I believe calculated risk is so necessary for both organizations and individuals to take if they want to develop.

However, the risk was exaggerated. It was mitigated by three factors; I have mentioned two. I knew the power of teamwork and the commitment of this team. They would adapt and correct quickly as they executed the plan. We also had faith in the four critical innovations we had put in place within the prostate center. It would be difficult for any competitor to follow and attempt to duplicate our program. If they did manage to do that eventually, we would already be far ahead. And lastly, we concluded that Vip was taking a much greater risk with us than we were with him. He was already proven, was leaving a venerable academic appointment, and his motivation would be its own force. All these elements proved true.

For ten years, Vip has performed over one thousand cases a year serving our local community, dignitaries and leaders from around the world. Risk is inevitable, but when all the dots are connected, the risk is much less. The investment in organizational capacity provided a real and sustainable return. It takes imagination to see it, but it's there just the same. The culture is the asset and allows teamwork to unleash potential rarely utilized, and facilitates innovation that is a competitive advantage. I love it when a plan comes together and the team in quiet confidence says, "We did it."

SAYING THANK YOU

How does saying thank you work to connect the dots? First, it is an essential role of the leader and a job only you can do. Second, it becomes a reinforcing loop, validating in words and rewards those actions consistent with the company's values. It clarifies what a win looks like. Throwing a teammate under the proverbial bus, or creating an end run instead of an honest dialogue, even if it produces a desired short-term result, should not be rewarded. Doing the right thing, the right way, for the right reason should engender a heartfelt thank you.

So, thankfulness becomes important both to the what and how of getting things done, but it's also a strong pull on the flywheel of The Big Why. In the process of thanking the team for the work effort or result, you must take the time to put those in context of The Big Why and connect back to the core. Some of the most artful work of a leader is finding ways to say "thank you" when the results are not there. It may be early in the journey and you don't want to declare victory prematurely or you might be off track and need to course correct. It is precisely at these moments that a thank you may be most important to bring people back to the why.

Initially, this might be a bit challenging to your leadership judgment. But once you start looking for these things, as I talked about in the last chapter looking for humor, it will show up. I barely noticed the Subaru brand until a few months ago when my daughter bought one. Now they are nearly everywhere I go—often two or three parked next to each other. I see them so much I have even started thinking that it will be my next car.

This is a learning that took me some time to appreciate and even longer to learn and commit to take action. Someone once joked with me when I was serving as chief financial officer that CFO must stand for Constantly Finding Obstacles. I wore that as a badge of honor until I later realized the deeper message. I was missing the opportunity to recognize and say thank you for the wins and good efforts. I was almost exclusively focused on what wasn't working in an honest effort to correct it. This was wrong. It was imbalanced, and it missed the art of leadership.

These learnings were reinforced when, sometime years later, someone would share, often emotionally, a time when I had given them an appreciative thank you or handwritten note during a difficult struggle to get all the pieces right in our performance march. I was humbled to learn that sometimes this love-based courtesy is the difference between someone giving up or intensifying the fight on behalf of The Big Why. Saying thank you is the last and best job of a servant leader, but I am even more humbled by the missed opportunities to authentically encourage and say thank you.

TWO CENTS AND CONNECTION

A regular counsel I hear is that you must adapt and adjust to your boss if you want to be successful. I understand the practical sense in this advice. However, I fear it normalizes the view of leadership and its role: leaders as the immovable force to be adapted to. The problem is that it sub-optimizes team members as individuals and the team as well. It is teams that nearly always drive innovation and breakthrough performance. I believe leaders who *lead with imagination* and who are connecting the dots work to adapt to those they lead. They work to discover what their truest capabilities are and help their people achieve them. It is a love-based principle and a potential for high return—a compelling win/win.

From this simple framework comes the most exhilarating and truest art in the work of leadership: creating a collage of the individuals you lead into a team, where each member is valued for their individuality and diversity while being committed to the best idea and success of the whole. The job of a leader requires learning to see the systems and structures of your teams and their team-to-team interaction, guiding it gently, and reinforcing its power as the servant and one who eats last. This is where artistry creates something unimagined.

It seems only fitting to close this section of the seven principles and processes of leading with imagination by going back to where your imagination began. There is a little book by one of the most gifted scholars on imagination, Dr. Seuss, called *On Beyond Zebra*. Let's listen in: "Said Conrad Cornelius o'Donald o'Dell. 'So now I know everything anyone knows from beginning to end. From start to the close. Because Z is as far as it goes.' Then he almost fell flat on his face on the floor when I picked up the chalk and drew one letter more! A letter he never had dreamed of before! And I said, 'You can stop, if you want, with the Z. Because most people stop with the Z but not me!' "

This is just a beginning. We don't know what is possible or beyond. Your imagination is the only limit. Welcome to "beyond Z."

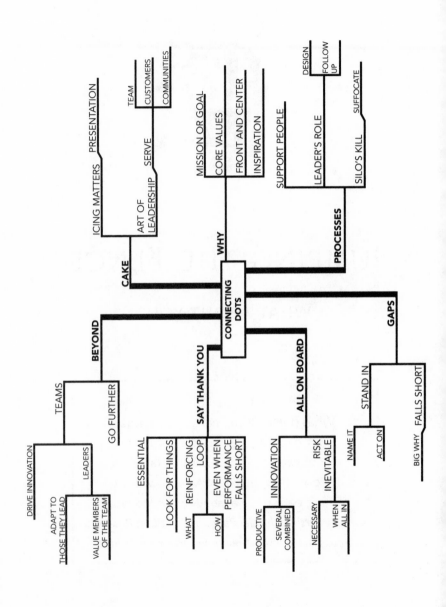

Jumping the Fence

WHAT ABOUT YOU?

Hold on tight a little longer
What don't kill ya, makes ya stronger
Get back up, 'cause it's a hard love
You can't change without a fallout
It's gon' hurt, but don't you slow down
Get back up, 'cause it's a hard love
Songwriters: Nathaniel Rinehart / William Rinehart
Hard Love *lyrics © Downtown Music Publishing*

LEADERSHIP LYRIC

CREATIVE CONCEPT: PRACTICE

Every artist, writer, musician, or creative person I know or
have read about invests in learning their craft and practicing
it. I heard a rock band joke recently that they have been
together for fifteen years, but they have only been good
for ten. While practice does not guarantee success, it is a
necessary ingredient to learning to lead with imagination.

SUMMARY

Leading with imagination requires three things: deciding
you want to, taking action, and constantly learning. Well,
one more thing: failing! And then repeating, over and
over and over again. Yes, it might hurt a little at first. And
in truth, it will probably hurt all through the journey
if you are continuing to grow in your leadership.

CREATED TO CREATE

If you have made it this far on our journey together, you are already engaged in beginning to leverage the power of imagination to make you a better leader, a better teammate, and a better person. However, you may be thinking there is a limit to imagination's usefulness for you. Perhaps you are saying, "But I am a businessperson. I do spreadsheets. I do analysis. I make plans. I close sales. I may be lots of things, but I am not creative. I get the benefit of imagination, but I don't see how it fully applies to me. I'm the person who makes the trains run on time, not the person who designs the train."

If that is you, I get it. I'm an accountant, not a musician, a songwriter, or a filmmaker (though I do have rich fantasies about all of those and more). Over time and thought, I have come to believe that God created us in his image. If we are created in God's image and God creates, then we were created to create. Even if you don't subscribe to God, it is still a very useful construct against the alternatives, and the evidence of human creativeness suggests something beyond us. Simply put, I believe that if this accountant can learn imagination and create, so can you.

Will it be easy? Probably not. Your challenge, simply put, is to overcome that six-inch divide between your ears. While it is one thing to recognize the logic and reasoning behind the views expressed and stories shared in this book, it is quite another to implement the changes that will be required to succeed in your efforts to unlock your imagination and navigate the intersection of imagination and leadership. It's not easy, but it can be done. I promise it will be worth it, and I promise it will be fun. The odds for success are in your favor, and once you experience it, you will never return to a world without imagination.

FOCUS ON YOUR MISSION AND A CALLING

Do you remember the Harrison Ford movie *The Fugitive*? Harrison Ford played Dr. Richard Kimble, a surgeon who had been falsely convicted and imprisoned for his wife's murder. Dr. Kimble escapes from custody and is being tracked by a U.S. Marshall played by Tommy Lee Jones. In my favorite scene of the movie, Harrison Ford runs down a drainpipe as he's being chased by Tommy Lee Jones. Ford yells, "I didn't kill my wife." Jones responds, "I don't care." Then Ford reaches the end of the pipe and faces a choice: surrender and go back to prison or take the huge leap into the water below. Harrison Ford chooses to jump.

To me, his decision made perfect sense. He could die from the jump attempting to escape. However, the decision to jump gave him a chance to escape. A chance to find out who killed his wife. A chance to clear his name and regain his life.

For Harrison Ford's character, the choice was clear. There was little time to analyze the probabilities. He had an instant in which to make his decision. I believe the choice was easy for him because he had a clear and compelling mission. He wanted to find out who killed his wife. Only one option allowed him the opportunity to continue his effort to accomplish his purpose.

Just like Ford's character, I have found that deciding to "jump off a cliff"—figuratively, of course—becomes a great deal easier when you are doing it in pursuit of a clear mission that you are passionate about. Dr. Richard Kimble had one goal, and he was willing to do anything it took to see it through.

The problem, for most of us, is that our choices are different than Dr. Kimble's. He had to choose between taking the incredible risk represented by jumping off a cliff or going back to prison. When the "easy option" is as unpleasant as accepting life in prison, the "risky option" of jumping is a lot easier to choose. In real life, however, the problem is that the safe option often doesn't involve immediate or obvious consequences—at least not on the level of prison. In other words, our problem is that we can choose to jump or choose the status quo, which masks like safety. There is, in fact, a real risk to maintaining the status quo. We are told to play it safe. We are told not to take risks or "rock the boat." The reality is just the opposite. Playing it safe condemns us to the "virtual prison" of mediocrity, like continuing to sail our boat with a hole in it.

What we need to propel us to a place where jumping off a cliff becomes an obvious decision is the clarity that Dr. Richard Kimble possessed. While engaging in true self-assessment and implementing personal change is never easy, it is liberating. Indeed, profitably so. As a first step in the process, take some time to consider your personal mission and calling. Are you clear how you want to spend your life? Are you clear about your mission? If you are not sure, one place to start is where you are now. Ask yourself, are you going to *work* or are you fulfilling a *calling*?

I calculated early in my career that we each have about ten thousand working days until retirement. If you are someone who is just going to work doing a job and getting a paycheck, you may think of those ten thousand days like this: "I have 9,999 days to work before I retire so I can really enjoy life." On the other hand, if you are pursuing a calling (*not* a job), you wake up thinking "Wow, I have 9,999 more days doing what I love. I am so blessed!"

Which category do you fall into? Are you on one end or the other? Most of us are somewhere in the middle. We feel a sense of purpose and mission, but we also feel stuck. Marcus Buckingham, in his thoughtful and provocative research, suggests only about 17 percent of us show up to our jobs fully engaged and playing to our strengths. If you are a leader, it is likely higher, but probably not by much, or enough. If that is where you find yourself, then the question becomes: How do we grease the gears so that we can get some momentum? And if we are leading people, don't they deserve to follow someone leading with imagination, with a calling, committed to helping others find theirs?

Just like Richard Kimble, it's time to jump. (Don't worry; we have come to the end of the Richard Kimble analogy.) Jumping off cliffs is dangerous. Jumping over a fence? Not so much. Fences seem to say *stay out.* Yet usually a series of small steps gets us nicely over and into new pastures. You may be feeling pressure. That is okay and normal. But I invite you to begin considering it not as pressure but as freedom to choose and an invitation to explore and imagine.

ORGANIZATIONAL INERTIA

Once you deal with yourself and the six inches between your ears, the next obstacle will be organizational bureaucracy (and if you don't work for an organization, you are still subject to someone's bureaucracy, whether it's from government, suppliers, or your family). Just as individuals tend to seek safety to protect themselves, organizations do the same thing. As organizations grow, they often develop an infrastructure that assumes a life of its own and increasingly focuses on controlling people rather than serving them. The result is that anything outside of the norm or that appears uncontrolled is questioned. Efforts toward change are instinctively and intensely resisted. Even great companies, when faced with an industry in transition, have a strong bias to resist those changes until it's too late. I imagine it's the same way white blood cells attack foreign agents in our bodies.

Earlier in this book, I discussed the efforts at Florida Hospital to fix the emergency department. Organizationally, we initially faced resistance to this effort. This was an example of organizational bureaucracy in action. Many well-meaning people viewed the effort as having a high risk of failure. Therefore, in an effort to protect the organization, it was suggested that, in this period of leadership transitions, we choose something easy that would more likely succeed and build some positive (though small) momentum. From the standpoint of the company, it was better not to try than to try and fail. Failure is bad, and we can't have failure, even though failure might well have been enormously valuable for the new learnings alone, in accomplishing a big goal.

If you do find yourself in a situation where the bureaucracy has you stuck and unable to live out your mission and purpose, then you will have a decision to make at some point. Should you stay and try to create change from within? Or do you "jump the fence" to an organization or purpose that will allow you to fulfill your mission and purpose? As Theresa Robinson writes in *O-Syndrome*, "The organization is clear about its purpose. Are you?"

LET'S BEGIN (OR STUFF TO GET YOU MOVING)

One of the easiest ways to start the journey is to be increasingly present and open to experiencing the space and world around you. Discovery is key, and most often it is accomplished by doing and observing. I was having a cup of coffee with a friend who is a very talented graphic designer who creates fonts. (I assumed all fonts had already been created and are available on my Word software.) He is one of only three hundred or so people in the world who do that. As he was sharing the passions in his life, he shared this quote: "Look to *see* rather than look to *look*." That is what imagination is all about. When you start to *see* things in one context, then you can apply or transfer that insight to another opportunity or situation. You will gradually, and then suddenly, start to make new connections.

For example, if your business involves customer service—taking care of people and creating great experiences—give yourself an opportunity to see and experience great customer service in action and really pay attention. Take your spouse or significant other for a weekend stay at a Four Seasons or Ritz-Carlton hotel or make the investment to take your family to Walt Disney World or Disneyland. And if you don't have a family, borrow someone else's kids and take them with you. They will see things you won't. Win, win.

Take the time to observe what is happening around you. Ask questions. *Is this what the process was designed to produce or are the results random? How are the team members engaged?* Pretty soon, you will find yourself thinking, *Why did they do that? How does that work? What is going on that I don't see? What is the process that supports this?* Let your curiosity run wild. Next thing you know, you will be that person asking both staff and customers game-changing questions that yield insight and wisdom.

Once you have been exposed to great service—and really paid attention to the process—you can learn from the experience and find new ways to do things in your business or life. The key is that you have to be present and learn to pay attention. The point here is that you need to take the time to open yourself up to new experiences. You will begin seeing a bigger world, and as a result, start living a bigger life.

One thing we know that sparks imagination and increases our observational abilities is altering our normal routines. For years, I have varied the route I take to work each day. If I go one way in the morning, I often take another way home. When possible—and when my Type A nature is managed—I will take a back road on a trip. One time, I exited the interstate on my frequent trips between Orlando and Chattanooga and explored the back roads of rural Alabama and Georgia. I saw a very different world than the one seen from the interstate.

Find new places to eat lunch. Act like a tourist in your own city and really explore the city you thought you knew. Try visiting another city and let it inspire you and expand your imagination. I have found that when I visit Washington, D.C., I think bigger while sitting on a bench looking at the Capitol, or the White House, or standing inside the Lincoln, Jefferson, Roosevelt, or Martin Luther King, Jr. memorials. There is no shortage of places to think bigger in this city.

Or what about Boston? Sometimes I think I am smarter just walking the streets between Harvard Square and Massachusetts Institute of Technology or browsing the amazing bookstores in between. Since I am in healthcare, I like to visit the Paul S. Russell, MD Museum of Medical History and Innovation at Massachusetts General Hospital or walk the Pike (main hallway) of the Brigham and Women's Hospital with pictures and descriptions of so many advances in medicine that originated at that institution. And then there are Nashville and Austin. I often feel another level of creativity strolling from one music venue to the next while absorbing the sounds and wondering about the journey of these musicians, singers, and songwriters.

And what about nature? This adventure can start on a back porch, backyard, or garden on top of your high-rise or on the window ledge in front of your kitchen sink. With this one, it is nearly impossible to go wrong or run out of places or spaces. I love the ocean. Some of my very best and inspired times have come from sitting on a beach just watching waves. But, equally, the Northwest seems as close to a heaven as I have been able to imagine except the pictures I have seen of Switzerland and the Alps.

Find your own places that allow you to *see*. Book a flight to somewhere you have never been and explore. Return to the places that produce both a grounding for your soul and a lifting of your sights. Make it a regular part of your "way." And do it often.

START A CREATIVE PROCESS

Another productive activity is to engage directly in a creative process. It can be anything from building a spreadsheet to cooking a new dish you saw on the Food Network. But I highly recommend something in the arts. When I left Florida Hospital, one of the first things I did was begin guitar lessons. It was hard and challenged every hardened neuropathway in my brain.

If music isn't your thing, then start writing for a few minutes every day. Enroll in an acting, improvisation, or dance class. Find something you have always thought about doing and just do it. Don't overthink it or, in my experience, your adult self will start talking you out of it. I often tell my kids, "Anything worth doing is worth doing poorly, at first." Then when I am acting too adult about trying something new, they enthusiastically quote me with a grin.

As you practice seeing and doing, you will start to make new connections and see the world in new and more colorful ways. In other words, your innate imagination and creativity will start a rebirth and continue to enlarge.

A final suggestion is to explore a concept called "mind mapping." Tony Dottino, whom I mentioned in chapter 6, shared this concept with me. It is based on the science that our brains are visually oriented. It turns out that the old phrase "A picture is worth a thousand words" is true. The brain is capable of remembering an incredible number of pictures with only a split second to catalog them. Walter Isaacson, the noted biographer, states, "Einstein wasn't far more brilliant than others, but he knew how to think better because he was visual."

One day, Tony facilitated an exercise with my assistant, Becky Villanueva, my able chief of staff, Lorenzo Brown, and myself. He gave us a visual mind map about a fictional person. It had all capitalized words, pictures of things like his kids, a boat, and new girlfriend. We had two minutes to study it, and then we turned it over. Tony asked us to recount the details about the person. There were twenty-five facts and we named twenty-two. When we repeated a similar excercise given in paragraph form, we remembered only eleven details. The difference was remarkable.

We adopted this way of thinking and communicating. Over time, this process of visual mind mapping was widely adopted throughout Florida Hospital, and even spilled over to the corporate offices. It was never mandated; it just spread. It helped us think better and kept us focused. It allowed us to "connect the dots" literally and visually. And, perhaps most importantly, it allowed our imaginations a freer space to *see* the whole and what was possible.

Shortly after that initial exposure to the power of mind mapping, I was flipping through the CD jacket of a musical artist I liked and saw the same type of map had been used to write the hit song recorded on that CD. Once again, the powerful intersection of the arts with business was compelling.

JOY IN THE JOURNEY

If there is one overriding message I hope you take from this chapter, it is to do something. Take a step—even if it is just *seeing instead of looking to look.*

In Brené Brown's game-changing book *Daring Greatly*, she introduces a compelling differentiation between being in the arena versus being a spectator. She recites Theodore Roosevelt's inspiring speech entitled "The Man in the Arena." Our conditioning often becomes the limitation of our own making.

We are often driven by our conscious and unconscious fears of what others will think or say about us or by our desire to avoid disappointment. What others think is "none of my business." Disappointment is simply a feeling. Acknowledge it, give it only the respect it deserves (very little), and move on. The arts give us clear language for how to do this: "Lights, camera ... action!"

A PICTURE IN THE HALLWAY

Al Weiss, the former leader for many years of all of Disney World in Orlando, is someone who takes action. In the lobby of Florida Hospital for Children at the Walt Disney Pavilion is a plaque commemorating Al for his imaginative leadership. You may recall from chapter 5 his desire to do something big for the children of central Florida.

That was the ignition for the extraordinary transformation described in chapter 1 from a collection of departments to a world-class children's hospital in just over two years. It became a model for Disney about the power of their influence and benefit for their surrounding communities. The clearest evidence came when we got a call to arrange a visit from Bob Iger, the CEO and president of the Disney Company. He was in Orlando vacationing but wanted to see what Al and the Florida Hospital team had done.

There had been no shortage of concerns from Disney headquarters about mixing the Disney brand (very happy kids) and magic with a children's hospital (very sick children). But when he saw what the Imagineers, the team from the Disney Institute, and our nurses, doctors, and staff had designed and executed, he was impressed. It was thoughtful design, engaging for the patients and practical for the caregivers. It was an experience for the children where they were the *main characters*. All of the scenes incorporated supporting cast from the treasure trove of

Disney characters such as Baloo the bear from *The Jungle Book*. He observed every team member engaged in the process of care and service.

What Bob Iger witnessed—and I am convinced the thing that wowed and touched him—was a transfer to our children's hospital of the Disney discipline, "It's not magical, it's method-ical," and the Florida Hospital mantra of love in all interactions. You don't need to wait for inspiration or a magical moment. Just act, learn, adjust, and act again, in a methodical way. Take a step, then another one. The magic will come, and the *moments* will happen more often. And you will be on your way to leading with imagination.

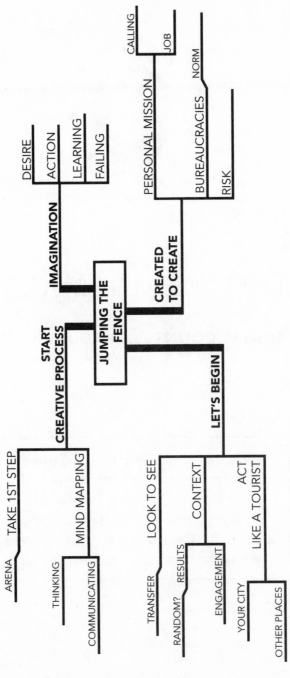

DIFFERENCE-MAKER

MAKING IT COUNT...LEAVING A LEGACY

"We are the miracle of force and matter making itself over into imagination and will. Incredible. The Life Force experimenting with forms. You for one. Me for another. The Universe has shouted itself alive. We are one of the shouts." —*Ray Bradbury*

LEADERSHIP LYRIC

CREATIVE CONCEPT: PERFORMANCE

Eventually every creator must take the stage, hang the painting, publish their writing, and connect their work with an audience. It becomes meaningful to them and others. They begin to create a body of work, or a legacy. They become difference-makers.

SUMMARY

It all comes down to this. The world needs heroes—lots of them, in lots of places. Your organization needs heroes. Your teammates need heroes. Your customers need heroes. Your family, church, and community need heroes. Your country needs heroes. Imagination is the superpower that gives all of us the possibility and the probability to be that hero. When you put on the cape of imagination, I promise you will be a hero, a difference-maker, and it will matter. You will release not only your potential but also the potential of all those you are privileged to lead.

WHO IS THE LEADER?

In chapter 1, I shared the power of *and* thinking. We *all* are leaders *and* followers at times. Doesn't it make sense to want to be better at leading and following? I have talked with many people who struggle to see themselves as the leaders they are. Moms lead children—and possibly husbands (especially if the husbands are better followers). My kids, at times, have led me. And as they have grown, there is an increasing balance of who leads and follows in our relationship. Teachers and professors are incredibly influential leaders. But I wonder what education would look like if they followed their students more often.

Leading teams is an intricate dance of leading and following. It may be the most important hands-on work in the art of leadership. If I have given the impression that I achieved the performance and transformation described in the opening chapter, let me correct that now. It was the dance we *all* learned to do, leading and following, giving and taking, asking and listening, trying and failing, loving and laughing. And that is just within a single team.

If the whole organization is to perform to its potential, then teams must interact with other teams similarly, like the living organisms they are. This is both the miracle and method of *leading with imagination*. Learning to *see* a team's dynamic system and structure and then opening the aperture to *see* the team-to-team processes is perhaps one of the least researched, recognized, and understood components of leadership. We should and can do better in each of those areas; however, it will remain the most complex aspect of the art of leading. If we do not develop our imagination to *see*, we will be destined to leave vast amounts of human potential untapped and on the shelf. While there is much to discover about this journey, one thing we do know is that it starts with each one of us accepting that we are leaders and we must lead.

One of the primary reasons I became so committed to launching a physician leadership program at Florida Hospital was based on my conversations with doctors about their leadership, or lack of it. Many didn't understand the importance of leadership. In fact, most didn't believe they were leaders. If they did, it was often a distorted view. They were unaware of how their actions affected the staff (whom they often did not see as teammates) or their patients. Let's consider that a stated aspirational aim of our organization was to help people reach their God-given potential. We interacted with our patients while they were in a place of crisis, often physical and psychological. Without leadership and imagination, we were destined to miss the opportunities to restore and perhaps advance their health and spirit. Indeed, every physician, nurse, and caregiver who walks into a patient's room is and must be a leader.

There are multiple studies ranking nurses as among the most trusted of professionals. When you are trusted, you are a leader to patients and their families. In fact, anytime you are interacting with another human being to get something done, you are a leader. I often reminded people that healthcare is a team sport. The moment we forget that, we get into trouble, and it will lead to hurting patients. Yet, on the flip side, when you combine the influence of the physician with the trust and presence of nurses, you have something special. Infuse it with love and now you have turned it into something extraordinary.

We have spent a great deal of time showing you (and hopefully, convincing you) that combining leadership with imagination is about the possible. Imagination is about *seeing* what others don't see. Once you can imagine the possibilities, it is about leading to turn vision into reality and seeing all the ways to do it.

WHAT'S IN YOUR IMAGINATION?

We all have passion(s) and purpose(s). One of mine is health-care. So let's have some fun imagining, and let's get a little crazy using the *yes, and* concept. Even if healthcare is not your passion, play along. Sooner or later, if you haven't already, you might appreciate what is possible instead of what is probable as you experience our current healthcare system. I hope you will build on this approach, apply it to your industry or interests, and explore a little with your imagination. So here we go.

I imagine a healthcare system that is both a catalyst for the community good *and* an economic driver, value creator, and great business. On the eastern edge of Orlando is a town called Bithlo. In a statewide study, Bithlo ranked as one of the most-challenged communities in Florida. It stood with nine-ty-nine other challenged communities identified by the study. In partnership with an organization called United Global Outreach, led by Tim McKinney, a local activist, we undertook to be that catalyst for this community. We intended not to take over or impose our thinking, but to come alongside in love and just help. Six years later when the study was updated, only a few communities were better off. Only one was no longer on the list: Bithlo. That is the power of *and*.

I imagine a healthcare system that competes for customers with resources and insurance *and* competes for those without. There is a well-worn phrase within healthcare leadership that roughly translates to, "No one competes for the poor." But what if we did? There are amazing and caring people all through the healthcare industry. They do their best to help those most in need of it. But it is rarely systemic, coordinated, or aggressively managed as a strategy. The odds are great that this lack of access for some is costly for society, more than it needs to be. Our approaches are mediocre as a process of care and leave patients feeling second-class and unloved. Bill Robertson, who leads MultiCare, a health system in Tacoma, WA, is endeavoring to take this journey. With some imagination, this could be a huge win, win, win.

I imagine a healthcare system that are stewards of their own resources *and* the employer's who choose to support their people with insurance coverage. My partners in CSuite Solutions specifically set out to find a proven, cost-effective model to allow every hospital system in the country, no matter their size or resources, to work directly with employers in their communities to accomplish this. It is about a direct relationship, transparency, accountability, and a shared mission of increasing each employee's capacity for health and well-being.. In this approach, the healthcare system leads with imagination by demonstrating how it works with its own employees first.

I imagine a healthcare system that is equally proactive *and* reactive. When I have an accident resulting in an injury, or it feels like my appendix is about to burst, I am grateful for the reactive and ready team in the emergency room. Most hospitals are pretty competent in this arena. But *proactive* might as well be a foreign country. It has always amused me how we call our current model of care *healthcare*. It strikes me that it would be more accurate to call it a *sick-care* system. So let's get on with earning the name *health*. *And* while we are working to that aim, let's focus on and integrate mind *and* spirit with the body. This work, using all of our collective imagination, creativity, and innovations, would truly transform us as a nation. Indeed, we could and should lead the world and reverse the trajectory of health on this planet. So much of the world's potential is locked up in lack of health or healthcare.

A few years ago, thinking in this challenging space led us to the creation of a partnership with the newly built Dr. Phillips Center for the Performing Arts in Orlando. We had a notion that an investment in understanding how the arts could support health, particularly our minds and spirits, would have a real payback. There are studies that connect the arts to reductions in health issues for seniors who are lonely, improvement in Alzheimer's, and reductions in pain, just to name a few. Creative expression is everywhere. It might be powerful medicine just waiting for us to leverage, with little new cost, to improve our minds, bodies, and spirits. I envision a partnership between hospitals and every performing arts center in the country. The possibilities are endless.

I imagine a healthcare system designed to serve *and* support populations and uniquely meet the needs of individuals. I have to confess: I barely have a picture of what this might look like. My friend Dr. Halee Fischer-Wright in her provocative book *Back to Balance*, might be probing (no medical humor intended) into this area with her thoughts about the need to balance the art, science, and business of medicine. I read the first chapter of her book early one morning on the beach and was profoundly moved. There has been something lost in the relationships between physicians, caregivers, and patients. It appears that the culprits may be the ineffective applications of science and business processes. And yet I couldn't help thinking that we have barely begun to tap the power both could bring to our sick-care and healthcare system.

This is a crazy and frustrating space where new ideas and technology swirl in both hype and reality. Words come to mind such as *blockchain, artificial intelligence, big data, predictive analytics*, and *the internet of things*. If we are imaginative and inventive enough, while keeping a people-centered vision in mind, God only knows how we might serve and the differences we might make.

SPEAKING OF MOM

In my role as a senior partner in a strategic advisory firm of former healthcare executives, I have had the privilege of meeting and working with people who lead with imagination. I received a call from Todd Park one afternoon. He and his brother founded a company called athenahealth. It sought to change the way physicians were able to practice by reducing the enormous amount of paperwork that inundates them. They had a vision: "Let doctors be doctors." athenahealth reshaped the information and medical record business and became the industry leader. Todd also served as the chief technology officer of the United States from 2012–2014.

Todd is motivated by a higher purpose to transform healthcare, saving our country untold billions. He and his brother, Ed, have started a new company called Devoted Health. It will offer what is called a Medicare Advantage plan as an alternative to traditional Medicare coverage. The overriding pillar, similar to their "let doctors be doctors" mantra, is now "Every member is mom." He told me, "We love our mom (and dad), and there has to be a better way to organize and manage care for our parents. We are building a company and culture driven by love."

I think this qualifies Todd and Devoted Health as superheroes of imagination. In the rough-and-tumble world of Silicon Valley technology and insurance, this vision is huge, and Todd's enthusiasm and passion are well past contagious. When we speak, I am energized and engaged with this endeavor, even if I'm just a cheerleader for it. I would bet my money on the power of love to fuel imagination at Devoted Health, and I would bet on Todd, his brother, and the imaginative people who have joined them on this adventure to love mom. I am grateful that they imagine a better way and that they are taking action.

GRACE NOTE

On a warm day in 2009, on a beach near Charleston, South Carolina, two friends went surfing, as they often did. Matt Alexander, an MBA with a background in strategy, and Ed O'Bryan, an emergency physician and faculty at the Medical University of South Carolina, began talking about a better way—a better way for people in the poorest parts of the world to access healthcare—get this—that most people could afford. By the time they packed up their boards and made the drive back into town, they had made a decision and were determined to take action.

They added another friend, Michael O'Neal, and began to build a plan to open clinics in Africa and Central America that were self-sustaining. This would allow these clinics to be replicated without ongoing donor support. They would focus donor support to open new centers, thus caring for more people. They were fueled by the belief that we are all created equally, yet we are not treated equally. They wanted to do something about this, starting with healthcare. Most people working in healthcare told them it was unlikely they would succeed. Michael, who today serves as executive director, shared with me that in the early days, "We had a plan, and we had hope." And while hope is not a method, in the right hands it does have power.

They formed OneWorld Health and opened their first center in 2011. They recently opened their ninth site and have an audacious goal to have twenty clinics by 2020! Matt, Ed, and Michael have led a very talented and passionate team who are attracted by this vision. They lead with imagination with a desire to be difference-makers.

In January 2017, my son and I had the opportunity to travel to Tola, Nicaragua, on a trip with OneWorld Health to participate in the opening of a clinic. They were joined by the band Needtobreathe, which, with the support of its fans had raised the roughly $225,000 needed to launch the new clinic. This innovative partnership has raised over two million dollars to date.

It was clear that the band was motivated by the same desire to be difference-makers by positively using their success and celebrity for good. I watched firsthand their complete engagement with the process and the people this clinic would benefit. They took time out of a very busy touring schedule to spend several days both serving and celebrating the clinic's launch. This is an imaginative partnership, innovating everything from how to raise funds to the delivery of care. And it's working.

GETTING SMARTER

It is a reasonable argument to suggest that as people, we are getting smarter (or at least more knowledgeable). In this information age, we know more than any generation in history. However, we are not becoming more imaginative nor are we keeping pace with our knowledge. We are driving a car at night, faster and faster, with the headlights dimming. Our vision under these conditions is in extreme danger.

We live in an age of science and cynicism. Imagination is already in short supply. Thomas L. Friedman, the *New York Times* writer and thinker, has suggested in his book *Hot, Flat, and Crowded* that we will not solve today's problems with our current thinking. My interpretation is that we have an accelerating body of science and very competent scientists. What we lack is imagination combined with leadership.

We also tend to lose our imaginations with age. This is reversible, but that is not the worst of it. In this age of science and cynicism, we as a society are losing our innate sense of wonder. All of this has combined to yield today's increasing polarization, with a mindset of "If you win, I lose" and a decline of civility and dialogue.

This is a difficult circumstance and begs our resistance. It seeks more light, not less. It demands a robust motivation, a higher calling, and a deeper purpose. It calls out for disruption to our current course and speed. It solicits love and imagination. It is why your leadership matters, and why we need more heroes.

REDEMPTION

Back in the early 1970s, Robert Greenleaf put two words together that seemed to be opposed to each other: *servant* and *leader*. Almost fifty years later, these two words still live together in different venues and are supported by a growing number of leadership experts. They are still challenging and are too often taught in a shallow form as external tactics without the internal character work. This is a distortion, with occasionally good short-term results, but it always leads to detrimental consequences in the long run. It erodes trust within the culture and in leadership.

The order of the words in the phrase *servant leadership* is intentional and essential. One must first be the servant before being the leader. I never said this is easy. Chapters 3 through 5 were heavily focused on that transformation and preparation for servanthood. What I am saying, is that once we have made progress toward being an authentic servant leader we must add one more collaboration: imagination. We can express it visually and as a mathematical formula:

Servanthood + Leadership + Imagination = Difference-Maker

This combination is a powerful equation. The application of this formula will transform you and those you lead. It works whether at home or at work, supported by the worthy goals you are pursuing and despite the real and perceived challenges you face.

At a recent Needtobreathe concert, Bear Rinehart, their lead singer, shared that while they "appreciate the Grammy nominations and other honors that have come their way as a band, nothing will compare to the day their first bus showed up." A recent *Forbes* article described Needtobreathe as "The best rock band you've never heard of." Over the years, they have built a large and loyal following of fans the old-fashioned way: one great show at a time. They tour nearly nonstop. When that first bus showed up, the band had been traveling together (and often sleeping) in a van for almost seven years. "You can't imagine that feeling when we stepped on that bus," he finished.

I found resonance in his thought process. While I appreciate all the formal recognitions, external accolades, and performance results we received and achieved at Florida Hospital, some of which I recounted in chapter 1, they aren't the biggest story. Florida Hospital is not made up of its people; it *is* its people. Leadership is about people, one on one, and one at a time, as individuals, each with unique potential. Because it's all about people, it's also a place with a 100 percent probability to fail. We are human, imperfect, flawed, and broken as people and as leaders. Despite this reality, we must still lead and do it with our whole self.

So the big story, the one that still brings that lump in my throat, requires effort to keep the tears as moistness in my eyes instead of a trickle down my cheek, and that births honest pride borne of an even deeper humility, is the nurse at the grocery store. I can still see her in her scrubs, probably exhausted from her long shift and eager to pay for her groceries and get home. Yet, when the cashier noticed her Florida Hospital name badge, she volunteered a testimonial from the heart, "I love my job," she said, "and I love working at Florida Hospital."

Despite all my known and unknown failures as a leader, that unsolicited declaration is the story. "You can't imagine the feeling."

It is redemption. It is the perfect result of the imperfect struggle to *lead with imagination*. As Frodo in *Lord of the Rings* asked his friend, "Sam, what is this tale we have fallen into?" It turns out, it is a redemption story, in other words, a love story. It is my story, and it is every leader's story who determines to *lead with imagination*.

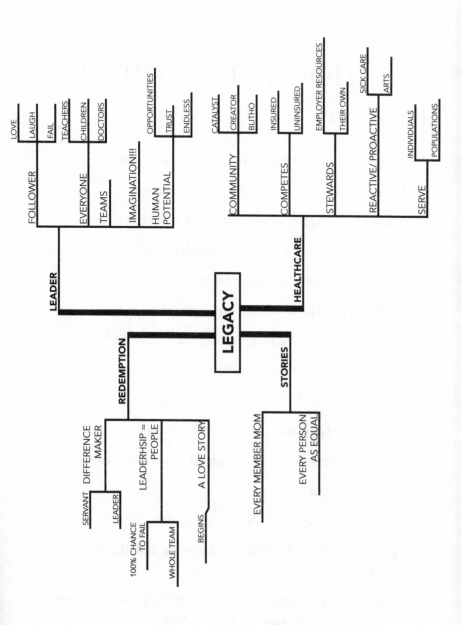

THOUGHT LEADERS

Chris Argyris – *Overcoming Organizational Defenses*

Brené Brown – *Daring Greatly* and *Rising Strong*

Margaret J. Wheatley – *Leadership and the New Science*

Russel L. Ackoff – *Ackoff's Fables* and *Ackoff's Best*

Sir Ken Robinson – *Out of Our Minds*

Robert J. Fritz – *Elements* and *Creating*

Gordon R. Sullivan, General Retired – *Hope Is Not a Method*

H. Thomas Johnson/Robert S. Kaplan – *Relevance Lost*

Peter Senge – *The Fifth Discipline* and *Presence*

Jim Collins – *Good to Great* and *Great by Choice*

Robert J. Anderson/William A. Adams – *Mastering Leadership*

Xenephon – *Anabasis*

Robert K. Greenleaf – *The Servant as Leader*

Peter F. Drucker – *The Effective Executive* and *The Practice of Management*

Sandy Shugart - *Leadership In The Crucible of Work: Discovering the Interior Life of an Authentic Leader*

RESOURCES

Sinek, S. (2014). *Leaders Eat Last: Why Some Teams Pull Together and Others Don't*. New York: Portfolio.

Merriam-Webster's Collegiate Dictionary (10th ed.). (1999). Springfield, MA: Merriam-Webster Incorporated.

Hertling, M. (2016). *Growing Physician Leaders: Empowering Doctors to Improve Our Healthcare*. New York: Florida Hospital.

Isaacson, W. (2017). *Leonardo Da Vinci*. New York: Simon & Schuster.

Brown, B. (2015). *Daring Greatly: How the Courage to Be Vulnerable Transforms the Way We Live, Love, Parent, and Lead*. New York: Avery.

Brown, B. (2015). *Rising Strong: The Reckoning. The Rumble. The Revolution. If We Are Brave Enough, Often Enough, We Will Fall. This is a book about what it takes to get back up*. New York: Spiegel & Grau.

Osterwalder, A. & Y. Pigneur. (2010). *Business Model Generation*. New Jersey: John Wiley & Sons, Inc.

Wheatley, M.J. (1999). *Leadership and the New Science: Discovering Order in a Chaotic World*.

Ghiselin, B. (1986). *The Creative Process: Reflections on Invention in the Arts and Sciences*. California: Transformational Book Circle.

Godin, S. (2008). *Tribes: We Need You to Lead Us*. New York: Penguin Group.

Wilkinson, A. (2015). *The Creator's Code: The Six Essential Skills of Extraordinary Entrepreneurs*. New York: Simon & Schuster.

Robinson, T. M. (2017). *O-Syndrome: When Work is 24/7 and You're Not*. Texas: Master Trainer TMR.

Meacham, J. (2012). *Thomas Jefferson: The Art of Power*. New York: Random House.

Buzan, T., T. Dottino., & R. Isreal. (1999). *The Brainsmart Leader*. Vermont: Gower Publishing Limited.

Green, K., & R. Green. (1998). *The Man Behind the Magic: The Story of Walt Disney*. New York: Penguin Group.

Ackoff, R. L., & S. Rovin. (2005). *Beating the System: Using Creativity to Outsmart Bureaucracies*. California: Berrett-Koehler Publishers, Inc.

Wallace, C. (2011). *The Leadership Gap*. Pennsylvania: Destiny Image Publishers, Inc.

Lencioni, P. (2012). *The Advantage: Why Organizational Health Trumps Everything Else in Business*. California: Jossey-Bass.

Fritz, R. (2000). *Elements: The Writings of Robert Fritz*. Vermont: Newfane Press.

Sullivan, G. R., & M. V. Harper. (1996). *Hope Is Not a Method*. New York: Broadway Books.

Greenleaf, Robert K. (1991). *The Servant as Leader*. Indiana: Robert K. Greenleaf Center.

GRATITUDE

LOOKING BACK ON A PROJECT OF THIS MAGNITUDE AND A journey of this duration it is daunting to remember all those who have contributed, specifically to bring this book to completion, generally who have influenced or lived out the ideas and stories captured in these pages, and who have enriched and enlivened the "seeing" and "support" I have so often needed. This is my best attempt, and it comes with my deepest apologies for those I have missed.

FOR THIS PROJECT
Tina S. Paradis
Clint Kreitner
Joseph Nicosia
Lu Anne Stewart
Ryan Paradis
– to each of you for your thoughtful manuscript review, insights, improvements, and support in the journey

Curtis Wallace – for imagining with me and every step of the process

Theresa Robinson – your energetic and spirited engagement

Jeff James – the push to start and stay on it, the reminder about the power of story, and the Disney learnings

Tony Dottino and Evelyn Walker – your integral role in the Florida Hospital journey and the fantastic mind maps

Harrison Wallace – for the edited mind maps

Bree Lowery – making all of this happen

Lisa Goolsby – great coffee and a plan

Show Don't Tell Productions – creative infusion and video storytelling

Justin Oeftger – a brilliant cartoon just in time

Billie Brownell – editing

Blake Atwood – editing

Scotty W. Smith –reminding me to keep imagining

Jessica Paradis – references and quotes

Brooke Paradis – encouragement

Trenton Thomson – laughs and the stories

Sydney Parton – reading the first draft

Teri Reutebuch – lending a hand

Olivia Harding-Londis Paradis – enthusiasm and always a laugh

Jonathan Lowery – doing what it takes

Stewart Schaffer – daily support

Alison Vicent – guidance and support

Michael L. Millenson – your encouragement and push for excellence

Jonathan Merkh/Forefront Books – taking us to the next level

Sanford C. Shugart – for your wisdom, showing a way, and a fantastic Foreword

Des Cummings – for every moment of inspiration, insight, encouragement, leadership, laughter, mentorship, and countless adventures in trying things

FLORIDA HOSPITAL SENIOR OPERATIONS COUNCIL AND CHIEFS OF THE MEDICAL STAFF

Philip Sanchez, MD

Tom Carson, MD

John Guarneri, MD

Yitzhak Dani Haim, MD

Edwin Wilson, MD

David Banks

Jayne Bassler

Andy Crowder

Sheryl Dodds

Rob Fulbright (deceased)

Josef Ghosn

Randy Haffner

Doug Harcombe

Ed Hodge

David Moorhead, MD

Terry Owen

Monica Reed, MD

Sy Saliba

Marla Silliman

Eddie Soler

Des Cummings

Lorenzo Brown

Adam Maycock

Tricia Edris

IN GENERAL

Brian Nase

Amb Robert Mandell

Sue and Mark Hertling,
     Lt. General, retired

Barry Tryon

Bryan Stiltz

Bert Miuccio

Wintley Phipps

Steve French

Jim Lewis

Scott Brady, MD

Steven Engel

Marie and Tim Kuck

Marjorie Thomas

Tom Yochum

Max Hooper

Mike Schultz

Mark Tumblin

M.J. Soileau and the

University of Central Florida

Brice Gramm

Niel Finkler, MD

Vipul Patel, MD

Ernie Sadau

Mike Gentry

Scott Wooten

Todd Werner

Timothy McKinney

Jonathan Ellen, MD

Todd Park

Halee Fischer-Wright, MD

Jon Johnson

Kathy Ramsberger

Kevin Jackson

Leeland Kaiser

LeAnn Kaiser

Robert Pryor

Jim Banghart

Sherri Sitarik

Yehuda Dror

Patrick Horine

Don Stillman

Cindy and Dan Blom

Tom Werner

Jeff Londis

Karl Haffner

David Ferguson

Kettering Health Network

Charleston Crew – Channing Pons, Matt Alexander, Mike Burkhold, Matt Gough, Tyler McCoy, Ed O'Bryan, Michael O'Neal

John and Betty Paradis (deceased) and Joan

Sara Alsup, Donna Burske, Penny Jones, Becky Villanueva , & April Navarro – support, endurance, and a sense of humor

Zak Keeney

Derek Morris

Reynold Acosta

Jay Perez

Geoff Patterson

Garret Jones

Brian Gottschalk

Scott Johnson

Tanya Swan

Pamela Hoelzle

Island Roasters Coffee, Third Wave Café, Café Verde (New Smyrna Beach)

Jack and Jolene Billingham, Ed and Gina Nelson (best New Smyrna Beach neighbors)

Lee University Library

David Russell and SAK Comedy Lab – for the memories

Stephen Curtis Chapman – for speaking to my heart so often

Drew Holcomb– for modeling a way

Ben Rector – the reminders in a desperate moment ("Fear" and "More Like Love" and the Ryman Auditorium)

Needtobreathe – for modeling the creative and collaborative process so artfully! Seth Bolt for producing Live at the Woods, the sequence from "Difference Maker" to "Something Beautiful" was the best pre-writing playlist one could ask for; Bo Rinehart for such consistent creativity; Bear Rinehart for pure passion sung into every lyric; and Josh Lovelace for conversations over coffee, a servant's heart, and the best saxophone throw in the business.

Grace Potter – a final inspiration

About the Author

BRIAN PARADIS

WITH OVER TWENTY YEARS OF EXECU-tive leadership at one of the largest hospitals in the United States, Brian combines concepts of systems theory, servant leadership, and the arts with his practical experience in finance, operations, and strategy. He illuminates a path for those who believe there is a better way to build an innovative culture, develop robust strategy, and achieve sustainable high-performance.

This is leading with imagination.

Keynote and Collaborative Conversations
The Purpose, Process and Power of Imagination
Seven Ways to Imagination
Creating Robust Strategy
Healthcare Re-Imagined

Brian can be contacted at imaginationworksmedia.com.

About the Author

CURTIS W. WALLACE

CURTIS W. WALLACE IS A LAWYER, EXECUTIVE, FILM producer, and author who focuses his unique background and expertise to enable driven, passionate people to use their talents to impact the world. Curtis believes that every person and organization was created to tell a story unlike any other. His job is to help people find and tell their story—that is imagination at work.

Curtis speaks on topics such as:
The Leadership Gap
Unleashing Imagination
Elevating Excellence

Curtis can be contacted at imaginationworksmedia.com.

CSuite
Solutions

WE ARE A COLLEGIAL GROUP OF FORMER HEALTHCARE CEOs who share core values and a common desire to significantly improve the U.S. healthcare industry. Our long-term goal with every client is to achieve the role of "Trusted Advisor" to its president, CEO, and other C-Suite executives.

Our mission is to use our decades of experience and expertise to assist healthcare systems to become risk- and network-ready so they can succeed in the new Value-Based healthcare frontier.

Link to our website at csuitesolutions.com for bios, services, news releases, and white papers.

imagination
WORKS MEDIA

OUR MISSION

TO ENLIGHTEN, ENLARGE, ENTERTAIN, AND ENERGIZE LEADERS to experience the power and possibilities of imagination, creativity, and innovation.

We believe all are born with a designed imagination and curiosity. We want to help people rediscover and then use it for the betterment of their leadership and life. We are committed to supporting leaders to unleash their fullest potential and the potential of those they are privileged to lead.

Link to our website at www.imaginationworksmedia.com for updates on authors, new book releases, speaking engagements, and workshops.

Our books are available for purchase at Amazon.com, Barnes & Noble, and our website.

For inspiration, updates, and to touch base with our authors, follow us on social media @imaginationworksmedia.